Marvelous Multiplication

Also in the Magical Math series

Dazzling Division

And coming soon

Fabulous Fractions

Measurement Mania

Magical Math

MARVELOUS MULTIPLICATION

Games and Activities That Make Math Easy and Fun

Lynette Long

John Wiley & Sons, Inc.

New York • Chichester • Weinheim • Brisbane • Singapore • Toronto

This book is printed on acid-free paper. ♾

Published by John Wiley & Sons, Inc.
Published simultaneously in Canada

Design and production by Navta Associates, Inc.

Library of Congress Cataloging-in-Publication Data:
Long, Lynette.
Marvelous multiplication : games and activities that make math easy and fun/Lynette Long.
p. cm.—(Magical math)
Includes index.
Summary: Presents a series of activities, arranged in order of difficulty, that teach the operation of multiplication.
ISBN 0-471-36982-9 (pbk.)
1. Multiplication—Juvenile literature. [1. Multiplication.] I. Title.
QA115 .L73 2000
513.2'13—dc21 00-020473

Printed in the United States of America

10 9 8 7 6 5 4 3 2 1

Contents

1

The Magic of Multiplication

What is multiplication? How do you write a multiplication problem? How do you read one? What are you actually doing when you multiply one number by another? Once you can answer these questions, you are well on your way to discovering the magic of multiplication.

There are four basic operations in mathematics: addition, subtraction, multiplication, and division. Each of the four basic operations can be expressed as a symbol. The plus sign (+) tells you to add two numbers together. The minus sign (−) tells you to subtract one number from another. The multiplication sign (×) tells you to multiply one number by another. The division sign (÷) tells you to divide one number by another.

The problems $7 + 3$, $7 - 3$, 7×3, and $7 \div 3$ are different problems that have different answers.

When you use the multiplication sign ($\times$), you can write the problem either horizontally or vertically. One hundred fifty-two times nine can be written as either 152×9 or as:

$$\begin{array}{r} 152 \\ \underline{\times 9} \end{array}$$

There are other ways to indicate multiplication besides using the multiplication sign. Sometimes a multiplication problem is written by putting a dot between the two numbers like this: $5 \bullet 12$, which is the same as 5×12, or five times twelve. You could write four times six hundred twenty-two as 4×622 or $4 \bullet 622$. Another way to indicate multiplication is by putting parentheses around the second number. For the problem, three hundred sixty-four times seventeen, write $364(17)$, 364×17, or $364 \bullet 17$.

You can write the same multiplication problem five different ways.

✔ Forty-eight times two

✔ 48×2

✔ $\begin{array}{r} 48 \\ \underline{\times 2} \end{array}$

✔ $48 \bullet 2$

✔ $48(2)$

Now that you know how to write multiplication problems, it's time to find out the names of the three parts of a multiplication problem. Look at the problem 17×5. Read this problem as seventeen times five. The number 17 is called a "factor" and the number 5 is also a factor. The answer to the problem (in this case, 85) is called the "product."

What are the parts of $9 \bullet 6 = 54$?

9 is a factor
6 is also a factor
54 is the product

Try a different format. What are the parts of $10 \bullet 2 = 20$?

10 is a factor

2 is a factor

20 is the product

Identify the parts of this problem: $6(111)$.

6 is a factor

111 is a factor

The product is not given.

Multiplication is an essential mathematical skill. You will use multiplication every day of your life, so start practicing and soon you'll become a multiplication master. Then you can proudly display the multiplication master certificate at the back of this book.

II

GAMES FOR UNDERSTANDING THE MULTIPLICATION TABLES

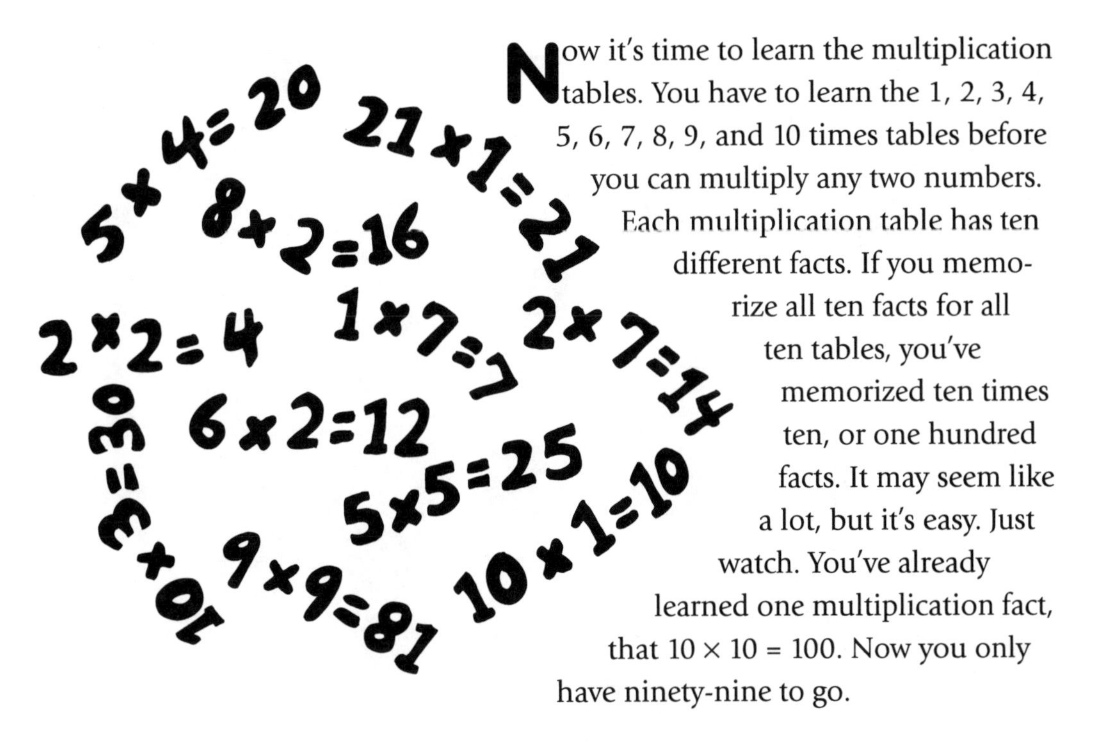

Now it's time to learn the multiplication tables. You have to learn the 1, 2, 3, 4, 5, 6, 7, 8, 9, and 10 times tables before you can multiply any two numbers. Each multiplication table has ten different facts. If you memorize all ten facts for all ten tables, you've memorized ten times ten, or one hundred facts. It may seem like a lot, but it's easy. Just watch. You've already learned one multiplication fact, that 10 × 10 = 100. Now you only have ninety-nine to go.

1

Can You Eat Just One?

Use ten tasty snacks to learn the 1 times table.

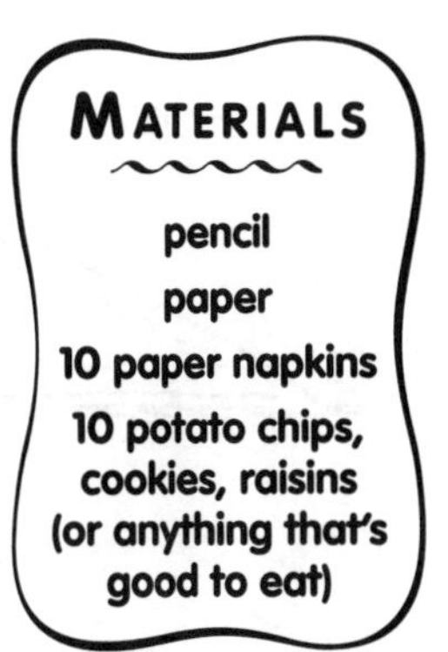

Procedure

1. Write "One Times Table" at the top of a piece of paper. Underneath that, write in one column all of the problems that make up the 1 times table, without the answers. Your times table should look like the one here.
2. Place the napkins on the table. On each napkin, place one potato chip, cookie, or whatever food you picked. Each napkin represents one group.

One Times Table

1 x 1 =
2 x 1 =
3 x 1 =
4 x 1 =
5 x 1 =
6 x 1 =
7 x 1 =
8 x 1 =
9 x 1 =
10 x 1 =

3. Look at the first problem in the 1 times table. What is 1×1? One times one means one *group* of one. Find the answer by counting the number of potato chips on one napkin.
4. Look at the second problem. What is 2×1? Two times one means two *groups* of one. Find the answer by counting the number of potato chips on two napkins.

One Times Table
1 x 1 = 1
2 x 1 = 2
3 x 1 = 3
4 x 1 = 4
5 x 1 = 5
6 x 1 = 6
7 x 1 = 7
8 x 1 = 8
9 x 1 = 9
10 x 1 = 10

5. Look at the third problem. What is 3×1? Find the answer by counting the number of potato chips on three napkins.
6. Now solve the rest of the problems in the 1 times table using the same method.
7. Fill in the answers in your One Times Table. It should now look like the one here.

Any number times 1 is that number, and 1 times any number is also that number. Five times one equals five, and one times five equals five. One times a thousand equals a thousand, and a thousand times one equals a thousand. The number 1 is the "identity element" for multiplication because if you multiply any number by 1 (or 1 by any number), you wind up with the identical number you started with.

So what is 1 × 1,365? Exactly, it's 1,365! And what happens when you multiply one trillion, three hundred billion, sixty-two million, three thousand two by 1? You get 1,300,062,003,002. Multiplying by 1 is just about as easy as multiplying any number by 0 (which, as we all know, always equals 0!).

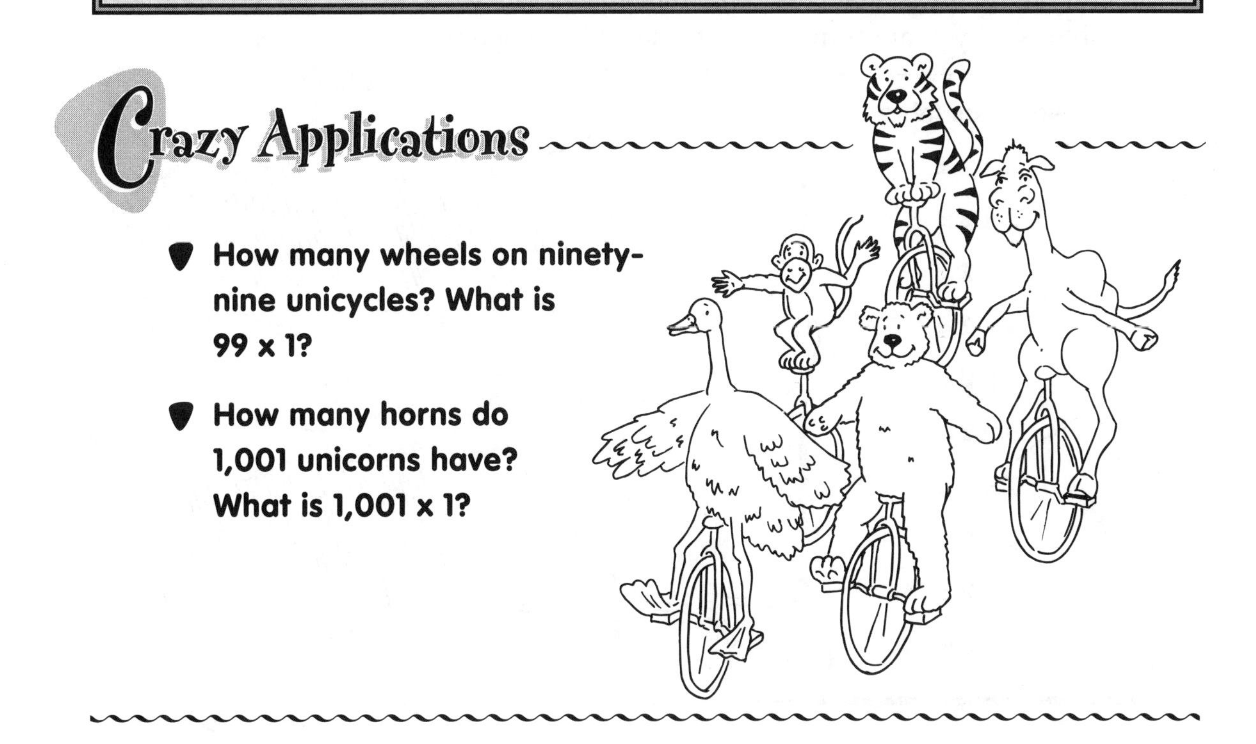

Crazy Applications

- **How many wheels on ninety-nine unicycles? What is 99 x 1?**
- **How many horns do 1,001 unicorns have? What is 1,001 x 1?**

2

Pair It Up!

Use ten pairs of socks to learn the 2 times table.

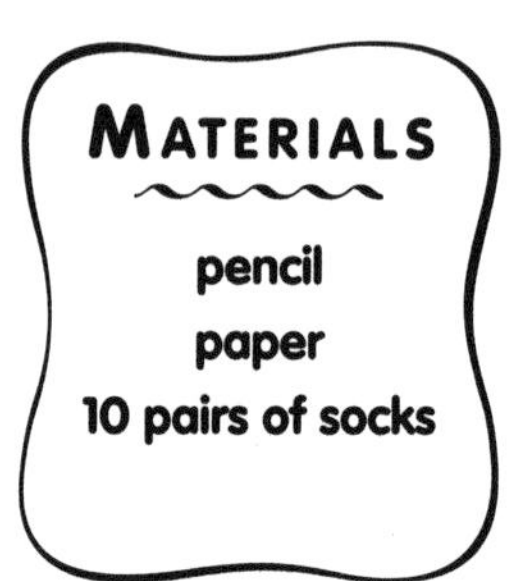

Procedure

1. Write "Two Times Table" at the top of a piece of paper. Underneath that, write in one column all of the problems that make up the 2 times table, without the answers. Your times table should look like the one here.
2. Go around the house and collect ten pairs of socks. Put them in a pile on the table. Now you are going to use these socks to figure out the answers to the problems in the 2 times table.

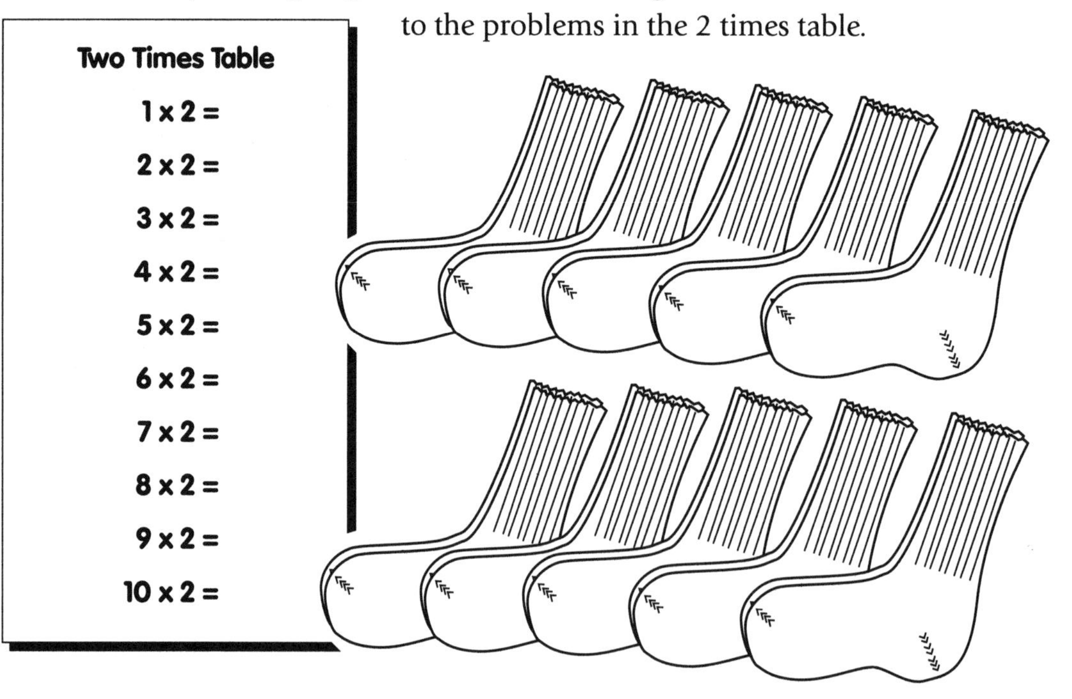

3. When you try the problem 1×2, ask yourself, "One pair of socks has how many socks?" Take a pair of socks from the pile and count the socks. One pair of socks has two socks, so $1 \times 2 = 2$.

4. When you try the problem 2×2, ask yourself, "Two pairs of socks have how many socks?" Take two pairs of socks from the pile and count the socks. Two pairs of socks have four socks, so $2 \times 2 = 4$.

5. When you try the problem 3×2, ask yourself, "Three pairs of socks have how many socks?" Take three pairs of socks from the pile and count the socks. Three pairs of socks have six socks, so $3 \times 2 = 6$.

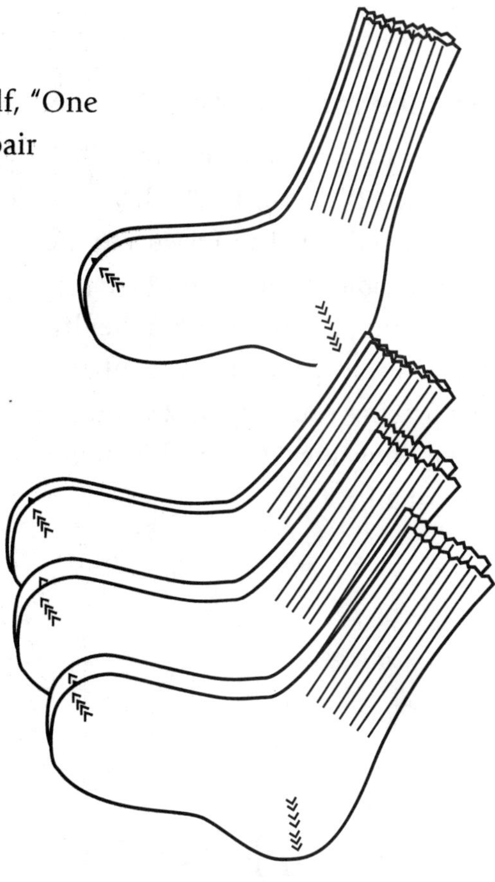

Two Times Table
1 x 2 = 2
2 x 2 = 4
3 x 2 = 6
4 x 2 = 8
5 x 2 = 10
6 x 2 = 12
7 x 2 = 14
8 x 2 = 16
9 x 2 = 18
10 x 2 = 20

6. Now solve the rest of the problems in the 2 times table using the same method. (Note: If you can't find enough socks, just draw little lines on another piece of paper to represent socks. You could draw 5×2 as *// // // // //*.)

7. Fill in the answers in your Two Times Table. It should now look like the one here.

Practice Makes Perfect

Read just the answers out loud: 2, 4, 6, 8, 10, 12, 14, 16, 18, 20. Did you notice anything? The answers to the 2 times table are even numbers. When you multiply any number by 2, you always get an even number. Just practice counting by 2's and you'll know the 2 times table in no time at all.

BRAIN Stretcher

If you had enough pairs of socks, you could figure out the answer to the problem 15×2, 23×2, or even 117×2. You can use anything that comes in pairs to learn the 2 times table. Use shoes, gloves, or even chopsticks.

- **How many eyes does a family of five have? What is 5 x 2?**
- **How many feet do nine dancing chickens have? What is 9 x 2?**
- **How many ears does a troupe of fifty-six baboons have? What is 56 x 2?**

3 Don't Skip This Activity

Use "skip counting" to learn the 3 times table.

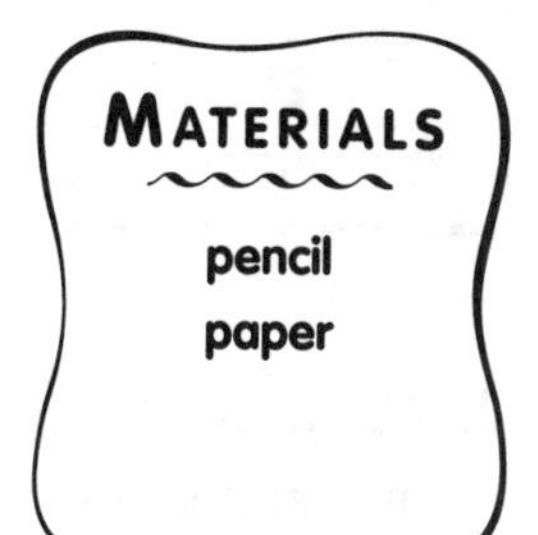

Procedure

1. Write "Three Times Table" at the top of a piece of paper. Underneath that, write in one column all of the problems that make up the 3 times table, without the answers. Your times table should look like the one here.

Three Times Table

1 x 3 =

2 x 3 =

3 x 3 =

4 x 3 =

5 x 3 =

6 x 3 =

7 x 3 =

8 x 3 =

9 x 3 =

10 x 3 =

2. On another piece of paper, make a skip-counting chart by writing the numbers 1 to 30 in rows as shown.

1	2	3	4	5
6	7	8	9	10
11	12	13	14	15
16	17	18	19	20
21	22	23	24	25
26	27	28	29	30

3. Circle every third number on your second piece of paper. Start counting at 1 and count 1, 2, 3. You landed on 3, so circle it. Now start counting at 4 and count 1, 2, 3. You landed on 6, so circle it. Now start counting at 7 and count 1, 2, 3. You landed on 9, so circle it. Keep going, and circle every third number until you get to 30.

4. Look at the circled numbers: 3, 6, 9, 12, 15, 18, 21, 24, 27, 30. These are the answers to the problems in the 3 times table. The first circled number, 3, is the answer to the problem 1×3. The second circled number, 6, is the answer to 2×3. The third circled number, 9, is the answer to 3×3. The rest of the circled numbers are the answers to the rest of the problems.

5. Fill in the answers in your Three Times Table. It should now look like the one here.

Three Times Table

1 x 3 = 3

2 x 3 = 6

3 x 3 = 9

4 x 3 = 12

5 x 3 = 15

6 x 3 = 18

7 x 3 = 21

8 x 3 = 24

9 x 3 = 27

10 x 3 = 30

Practice Makes Perfect

Place two cups and thirty pennies on the table. Put a third cup directly in front of you. Starting with the first cup, put one penny in each cup and count up the total number of pennies in your head. Whenever you place a penny in the cup directly in front of you, say the number of the penny out loud. The numbers you say out loud represent the multiples of 3. When you're done, empty the pennies onto the table and start again. Practice makes perfect.

You can use the skip-counting method to put together the multiplication table for any number up to 10. Make a skip-counting chart like the one in step 2, writing the numbers 1 to 100. If you want to put together the 5 times table, circle every fifth number. For the 7 times table, circle every seventh number. If you are solving a multiplication problem and you need to know what 7×6 is, just make a skip-counting chart in the corner of your paper and circle every sixth number. When you get to the seventh circle, you've found the answer.

Crazy Applications

- How many corners do five triangles have? What is 5 x 3?
- How many wheels do eight tricycles have? What is 8 x 3?
- How many heads are there on ten three-headed monsters? What is 10 x 3?

4

Counting Corners

Use ten squares to learn the 4 times table.

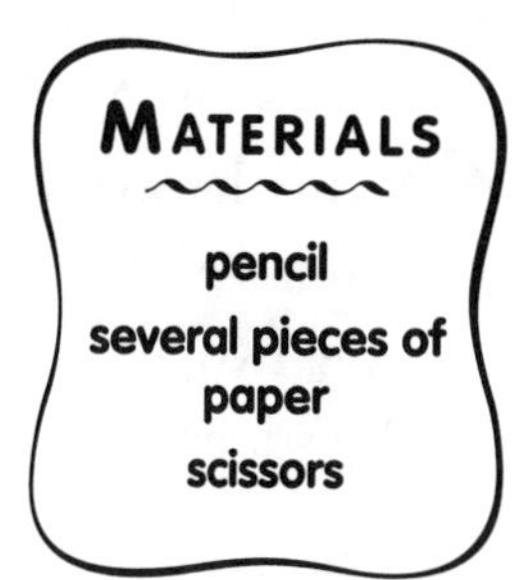

Procedure

1. Write "Four Times Table" at the top of a piece of paper. Underneath that, write in one column all of the problems that make up the 4 times table, without the answers. Your times table should look like the one here.

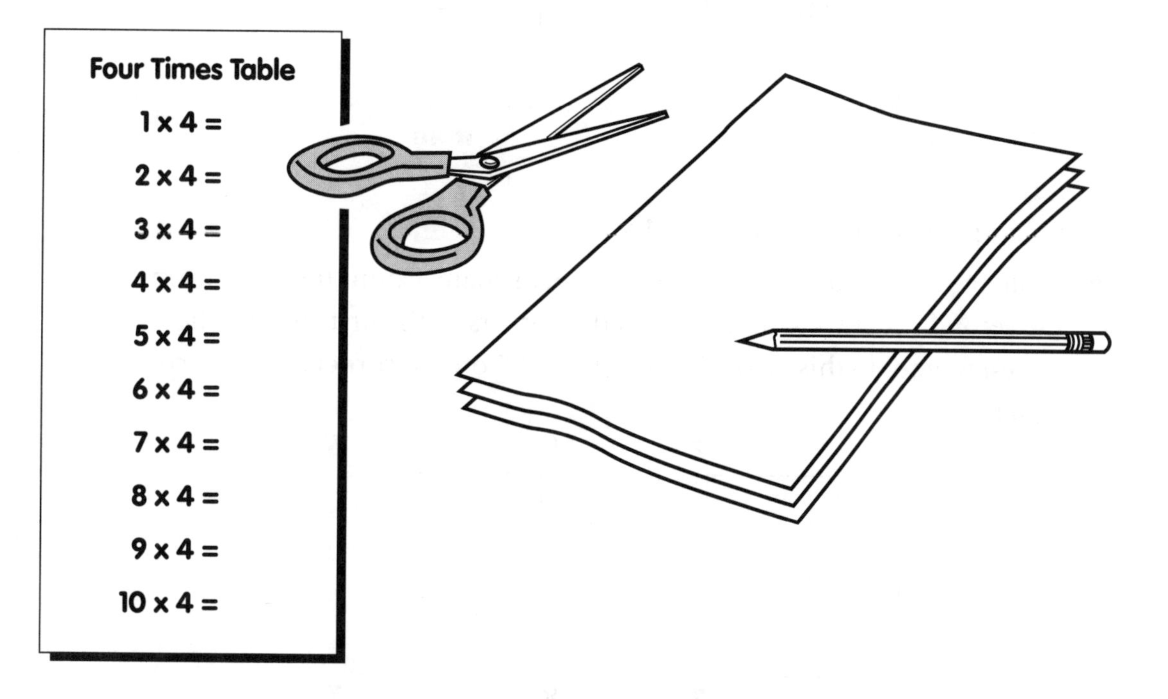

2. A square is a special shape. It has four sides and four corners. Each of the four sides of a square is exactly the same size. Each of the four angles of a square is exactly 90 degrees. The sides of a square can be any size as long as all four are exactly the same size. Here is a square.

3. Cut out ten squares. The squares can be any size as long as they are big enough to write on. Three by three inches would be ideal.
4. Write the word *one* on the back of one of the squares. This is the first square. Now turn the square over and count the corners. The square has one, two, three, four corners. Place a big 4 in the middle of the front of the square.

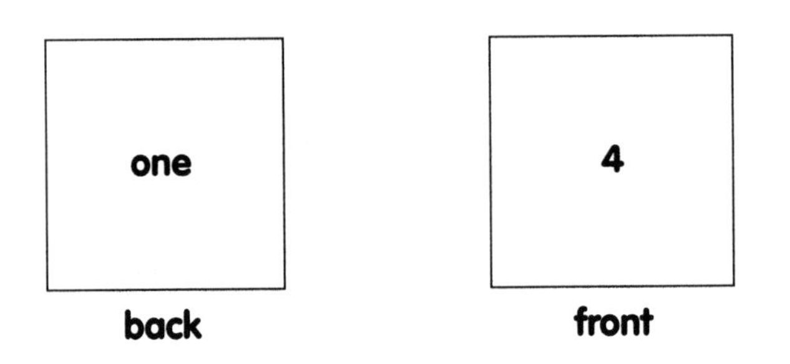

One square has four corners, so $1 \times 4 = 4$.

5. Write the word *two* on the back of another square. Count the corners on the second square and add them to the corners of the first square. The easiest way to do this is to start counting at 5 on the corners of the second square.

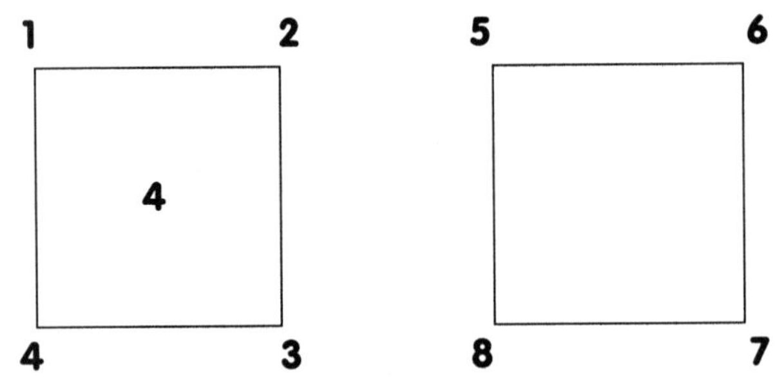

Now put a big 8 in the center of the front of the second square.

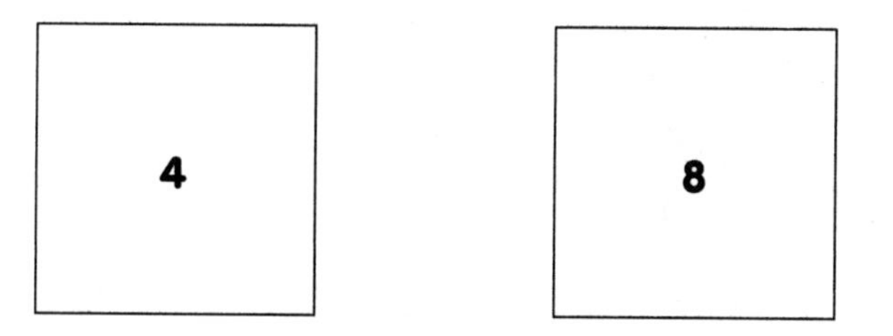

Two squares have eight corners, so $2 \times 4 = 8$.

6. Write the word *three* on the back of the third square. Count the corners on the third square and add them to the corners of the first two squares. To do this, start counting at 9 on the corners of the third square. Now put a big 12 on the back of the third square.

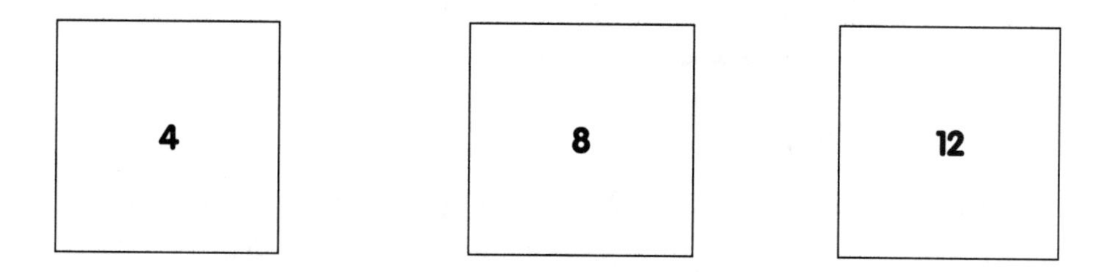

Three squares have twelve corners, so $3 \times 4 = 12$.

7. Label the back of the remaining squares with the words *four, five, six, seven, eight, nine,* and *ten.* Count the corners as before and put the totals on the front of these squares.

8. Look at the numbers on the front of the squares: 4, 8, 12, 16, 20, 24, 28, 32, 36, 40. These are the answers to the problems in the 4 times table. See, $1 \times 4 = 4$, $2 \times 4 = 8$, $3 \times 4 = 12$, and so on.

9. Fill in the answers in your Four Times Table. It should now look like the one here.

Four Times Table
$1 \times 4 = 4$
$2 \times 4 = 8$
$3 \times 4 = 12$
$4 \times 4 = 16$
$5 \times 4 = 20$
$6 \times 4 = 24$
$7 \times 4 = 28$
$8 \times 4 = 32$
$9 \times 4 = 36$
$10 \times 4 = 40$

Practice Makes Perfect

You can use your squares as flash cards. Mix them up and place them on the table so that the written words are all faceup. Draw a card. Suppose the word is *five*. Now you have to figure out what 5×4 is. Take a guess. Turn the square over to see if you're right. The number 20 should be on the other side of the square, because $5 \times 4 = 20$.

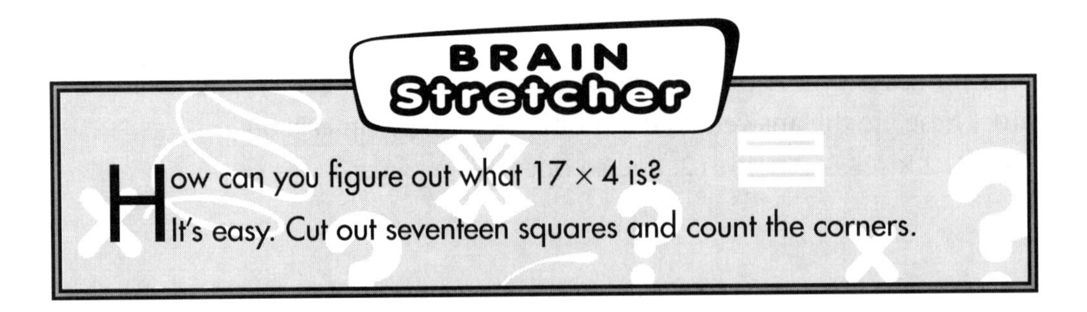

How can you figure out what 17×4 is?

It's easy. Cut out seventeen squares and count the corners.

Crazy Applications

- How many tires do five jeeps have? What is 5 x 4?
- How many legs are on ten tame tigers sitting on ten tippy chairs? What is 10 x 4 (tiger legs) + 10 x 4 (chair legs)?

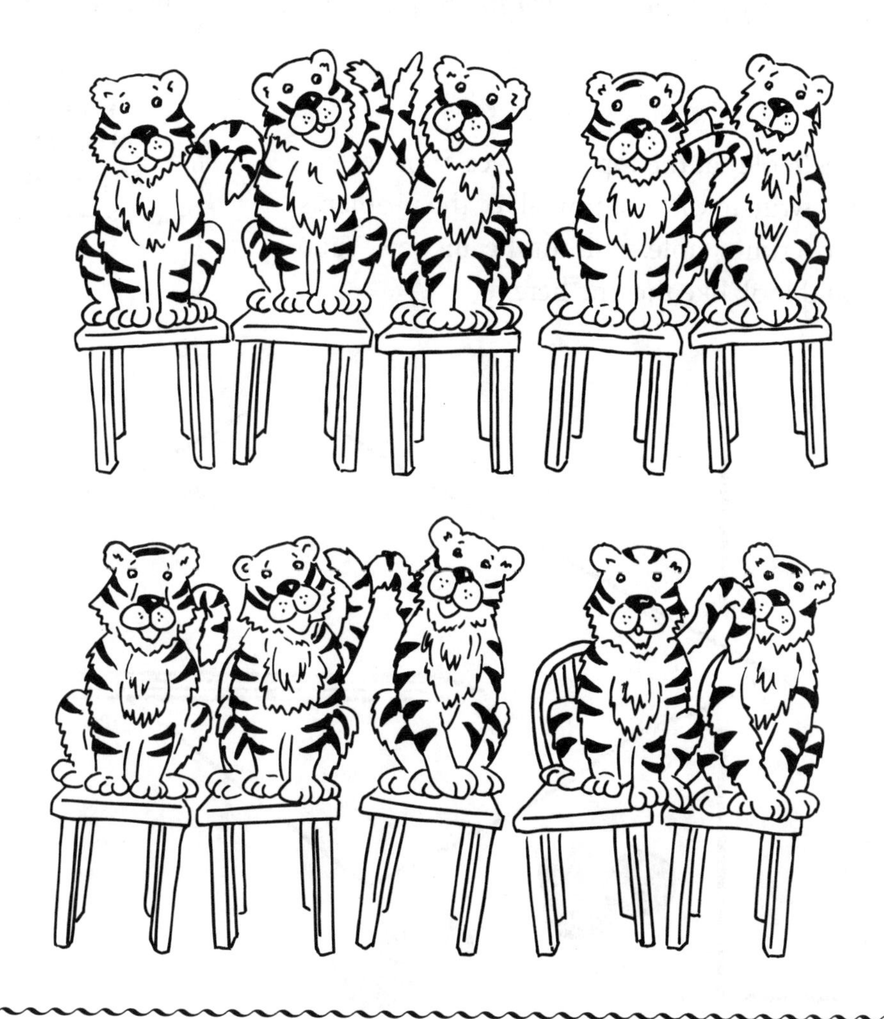

Nickel Mania

Use ten nickels and fifty pennies to learn the 5 times table.

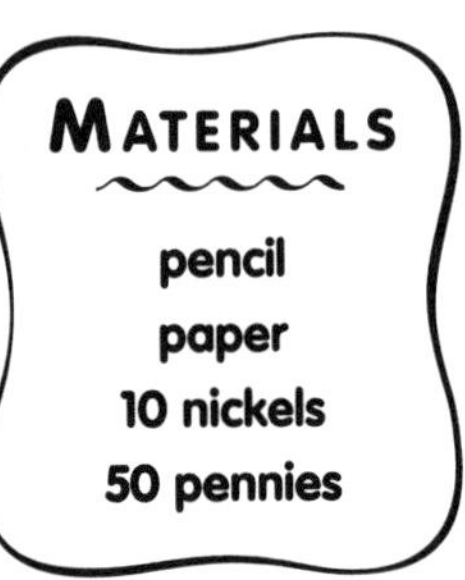

MATERIALS

pencil
paper
10 nickels
50 pennies

Procedure

1. Write "Five Times Table" at the top of a piece of paper. Underneath that, write in one column all of the problems that make up the 5 times table, without the answers. Your times table should look like the one here.

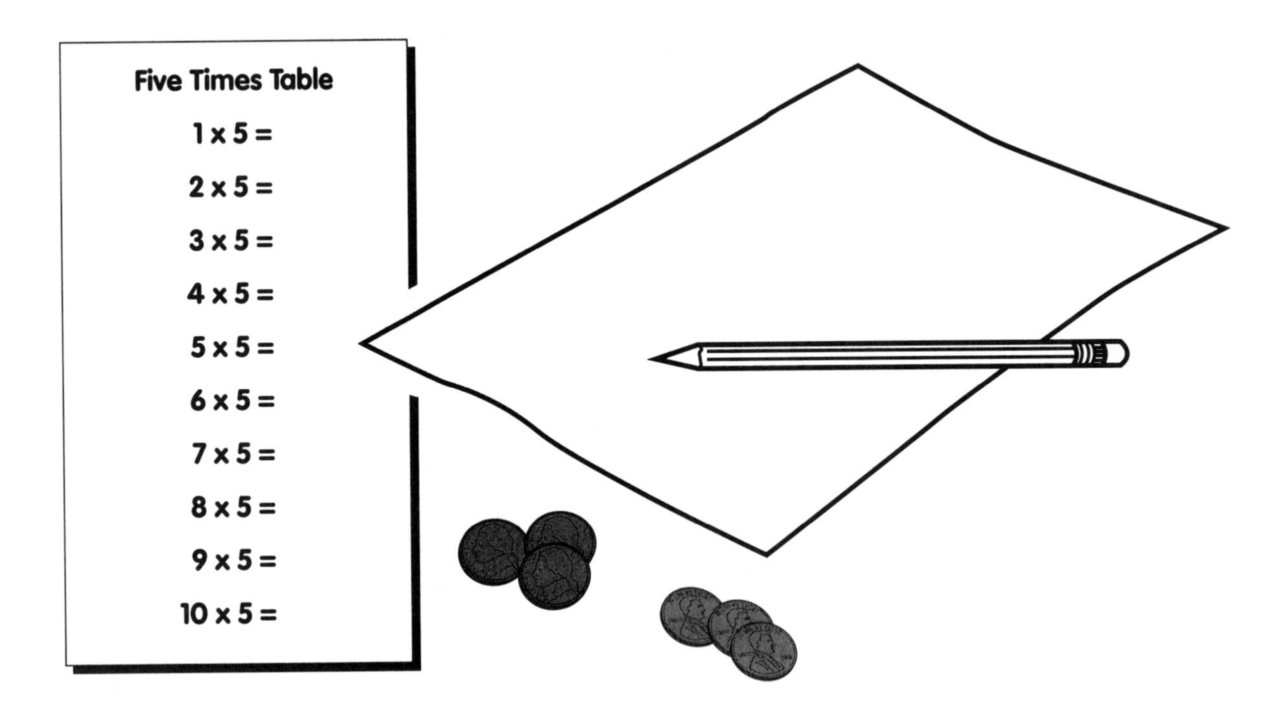

2. A nickel is exactly 5¢, which is five pennies. You can figure out the entire 5 times table by using nickels and trading the nickels in each problem for five pennies. The problem 1×5 is one group of five, or one nickel. Exchange one nickel for its equivalent in pennies. How many pennies do you get? The answer is 5, $1 \times 5 = 5$.

3. The problem 2×5 is two groups of five, which is two nickels. Exchange two nickels for pennies. How many pennies do you get? The answer is 10, so $2 \times 5 = 10$.

4. The problem 3×5 is three groups of five, which is three nickels. Exchange three nickels for pennies. How many pennies do you get? The answer is 15, so $3 \times 5 = 15$.

5. Now solve the rest of the problems in the 5 times table using nickels and pennies.

6. Fill in the answers in your Five Times Table. It should now look like the one here.

Five Times Table

1 x 5 = 5

2 x 5 = 10

3 x 5 = 15

4 x 5 = 20

5 x 5 = 25

6 x 5 = 30

7 x 5 = 35

8 x 5 = 40

9 x 5 = 45

10 x 5 = 50

Practice Makes Perfect

Use the nickels to practice counting by 5's. Drop the first nickel on the table and shout, "Five!" Drop the second nickel and shout, "Ten!" Drop the third nickel and shout, "Fifteen!" Keep going until you get all the way to 50. The fastest way to learn the 5 times table is to count to 50 by 5's. The nickels should help. As soon you can chant 5, 10, 15, 20, 25, 30, 35, 40, 45, 50, you've got it.

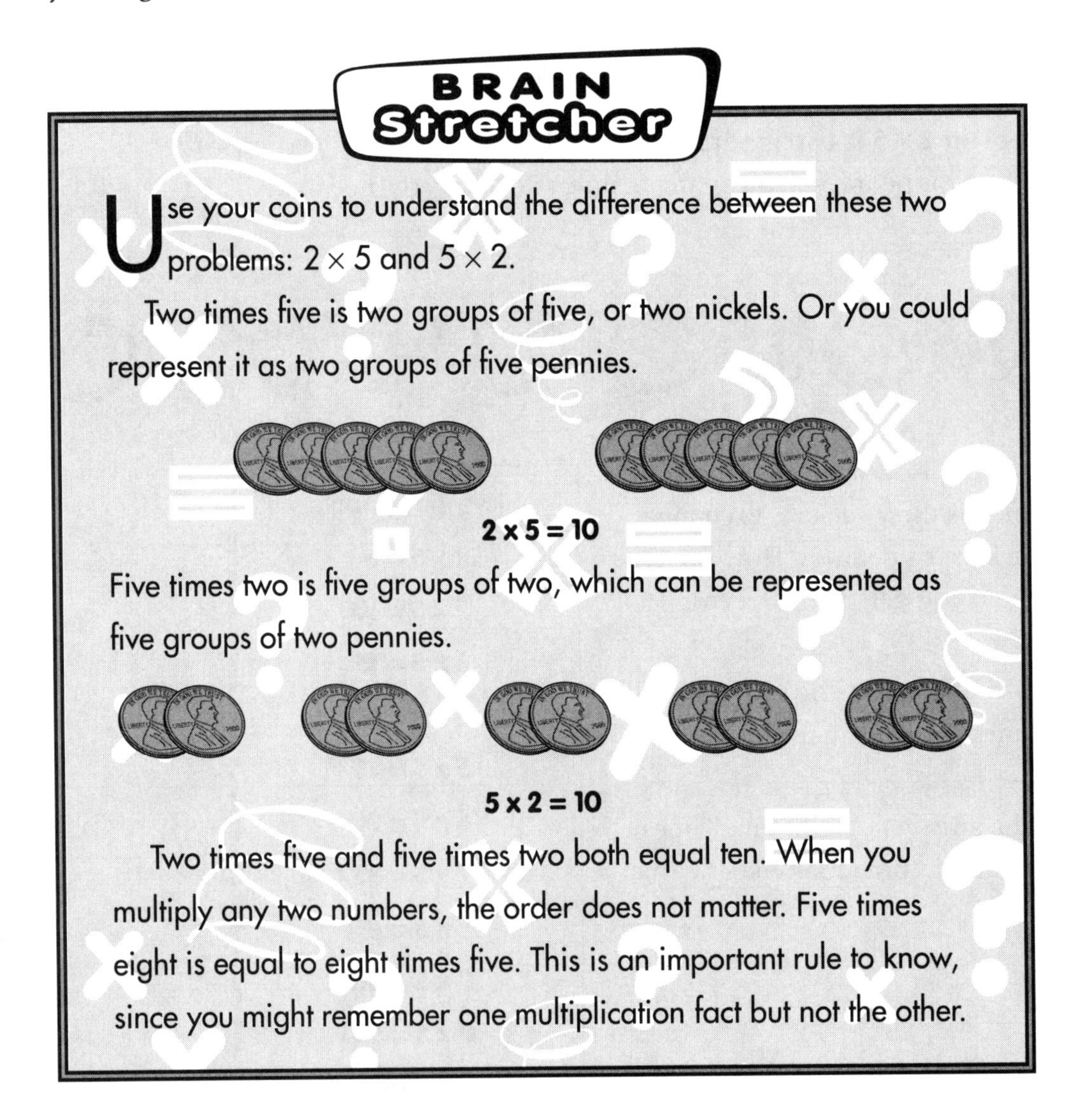

BRAIN Stretcher

Use your coins to understand the difference between these two problems: 2×5 and 5×2.

Two times five is two groups of five, or two nickels. Or you could represent it as two groups of five pennies.

2 x 5 = 10

Five times two is five groups of two, which can be represented as five groups of two pennies.

5 x 2 = 10

Two times five and five times two both equal ten. When you multiply any two numbers, the order does not matter. Five times eight is equal to eight times five. This is an important rule to know, since you might remember one multiplication fact but not the other.

Crazy Applications

- If a cranky crocodile has five toes on each foot, how many toes does it have altogether? What is 4 x 5?
- How many toes do two cranky crocodiles have? What is 8 x 5?

6

Tallying Toothpicks

Use 60 toothpicks to learn the 6 times table.

Procedure

1. Write "Six Times Table" at the top of a piece of paper. Underneath that, write in one column all of the problems that make up the 6 times table, without the answers. Your times table should look like the one here.

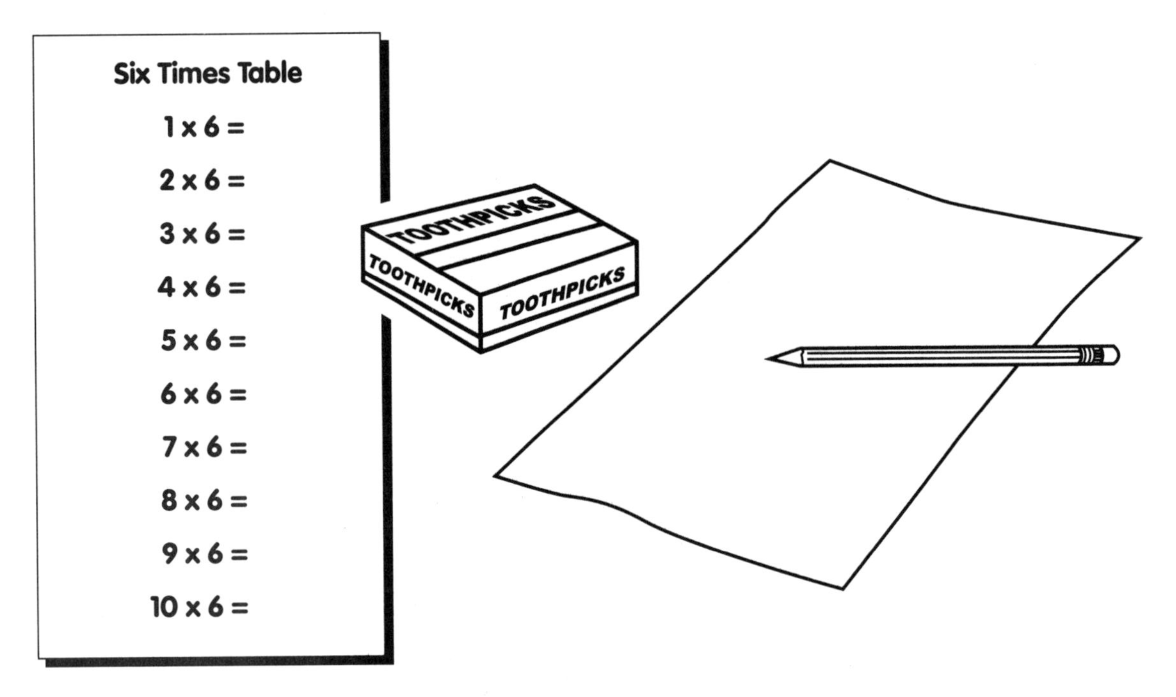

Six Times Table

1 x 6 =

2 x 6 =

3 x 6 =

4 x 6 =

5 x 6 =

6 x 6 =

7 x 6 =

8 x 6 =

9 x 6 =

10 x 6 =

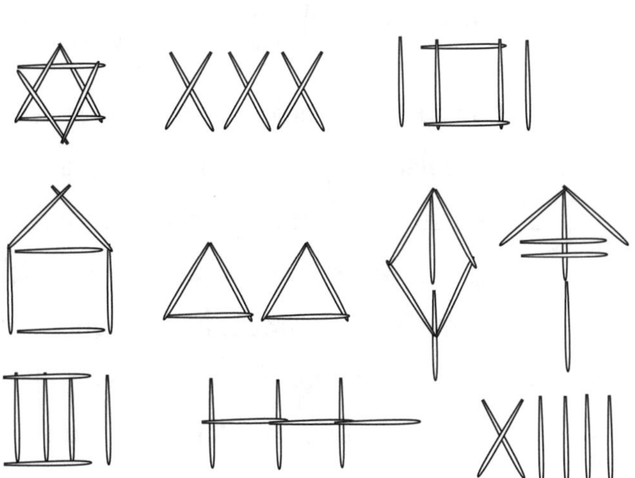

2. Make ten piles of toothpicks with six toothpicks in each pile. If you want you can arrange each pile in a creative design. Each of these designs contains six toothpicks.
3. Figure out the answer to the problem 1×6. One times six is one group of six, so count the toothpicks in one pile. There are six toothpicks, so $1 \times 6 = 6$.
4. What is 2×6? Two times six is two groups of six, so count the toothpicks in two piles. There are twelve toothpicks, so $2 \times 6 = 12$.
5. To figure out 3×6, count the toothpicks in three piles.
6. Now solve the rest of the problems in the 6 times table using the same method.
7. Fill in the answers in your Six Times Table. It should now look like the one here.

Six Times Table

1 x 6 = 6
2 x 6 = 12
3 x 6 = 18
4 x 6 = 24
5 x 6 = 30
6 x 6 = 36
7 x 6 = 42
8 x 6 = 48
9 x 6 = 54
10 x 6 = 60

Practice Makes Perfect

Write each multiple of 6 on a small slip of paper: 6, 12, 18, 24, 30, 36, 42, 48, 54, 60. Fold the slips so you cannot see the numbers, then place them in a bowl. Draw one slip of paper out of the bowl and see if you can state the problem that matches the answer. If you draw the paper that with 36 on it, you would say, "Six times six." If you have trouble, look at your Six Times Table.

You can use a box of toothpicks to solve any multiplication problem. Suppose you were asked to solve the problem 3×17. Just think of this problem as three groups of seventeen toothpicks. Make three groups of toothpicks and put seventeen toothpicks in each group. Now count all the toothpicks. You should have fifty-one toothpicks, because $3 \times 17 = 51$.

Now use your box of toothpicks to solve the following problems:

1. What is 6×12?
2. What is 11×4?
3. What is 6×16?
4. What is 11×11?

Crazy Applications

- **How many sides do six stop signs have? What is 6 x 6?**
- **How many legs do ten ants have? What is 10 x 6?**

7 Calculating Sevens

Use the addition function on a calculator to learn the 7 times table.

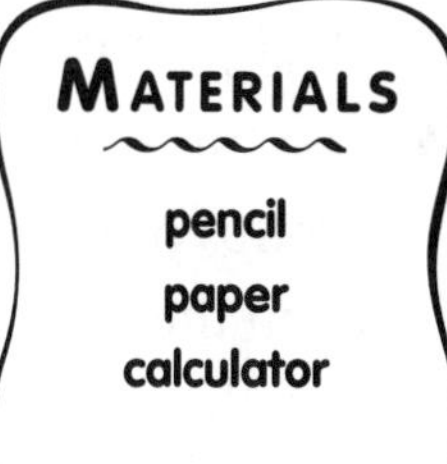

Procedure

1. Write "Seven Times Table" at the top of a piece of paper. Underneath that, write in one column all of the problems that make up the 7 times table, without the answers. Your times table should look like the one here.

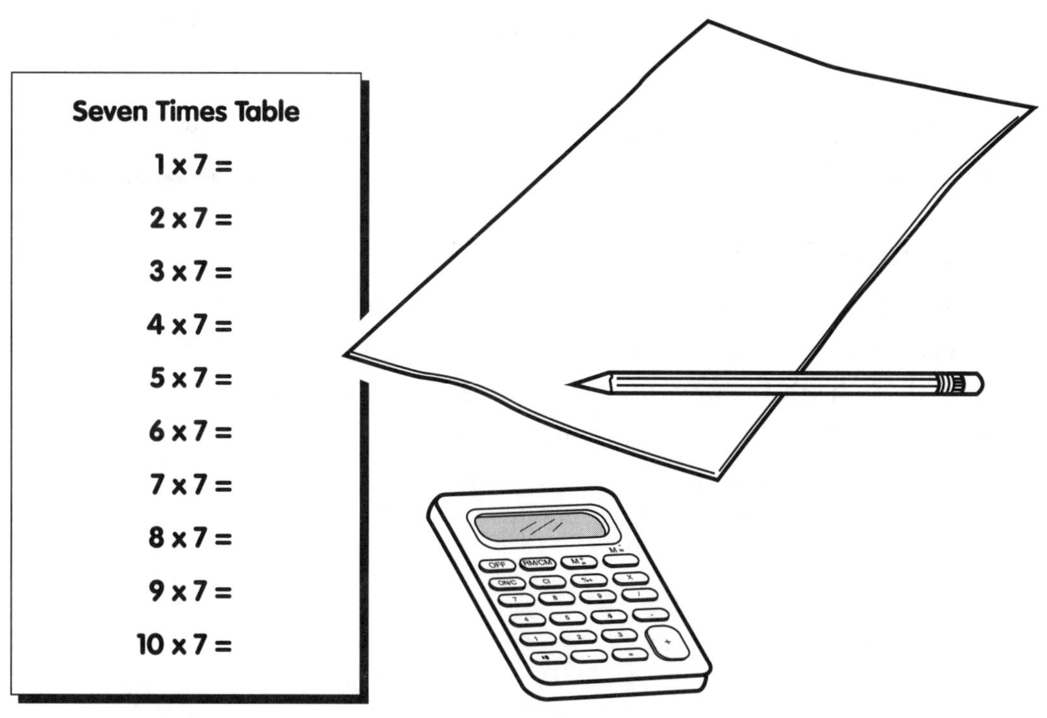

2. The first problem is 1×7, which actually means one group of seven. Push the 7 key on your calculator and then push +. The screen of the calculator should still read 7, because $1 \times 7 = 7$.
3. The second problem is 2×7, which means two groups of seven. With the 7 still on the screen from the last problem, push +, push the 7 key, and then push + again. The screen should now read 14, because $2 \times 7 = 14$. Don't clear your calculator, just keep going.
4. The third problem is 3×7, which means three groups of seven. With the 14 still on the screen from the last problem, push the +, push the 7 key, and then push + again. The screen should now read 21, because $3 \times 7 = 21$. You are solving each problem by adding 7 to the answer to the problem before it. Multiplication is often called "repeated addition."
5. Keep adding 7 on the calculator to find answers to the rest of the problems in the 7 times table.
6. Fill in the answers in your Seven Times Table. It should now look like the one here.

Seven Times Table
1 x 7 = 7
2 x 7 = 14
3 x 7 = 21
4 x 7 = 28
5 x 7 = 35
6 x 7 = 42
7 x 7 = 49
8 x 7 = 56
9 x 7 = 63
10 x 7 = 70

Practice Makes Perfect

The 7 times table can be a difficult table to learn. Use ten index cards to make a set of flash cards. On one side of each card, write one problem. On the other side, write the answer. Practice the 7 times table several times a day using these cards. Remember, practice makes perfect.

You can use the calculator method to solve a variety of times table problems. What if you wanted to figure out the 25 times table? The 25 times table is a useful one to know. It comes in handy when you're adding quarters. One quarter is 25¢; two quarters (2 × 25) are 50¢; three quarters (3 × 25) are 75¢; four quarters (4 × 25) are $1; five quarters (5 × 25) are $1.25; six quarters (6 × 25) are $1.50; seven quarters (7 × 25) are $1.75; eight quarters (8 × 25) are $2; nine quarters (9 × 25) are $2.25; ten quarters (10 × 25) are $2.50. If you calculate and memorize the 25 times table, you will be able to count change in no time.

Crazy Application

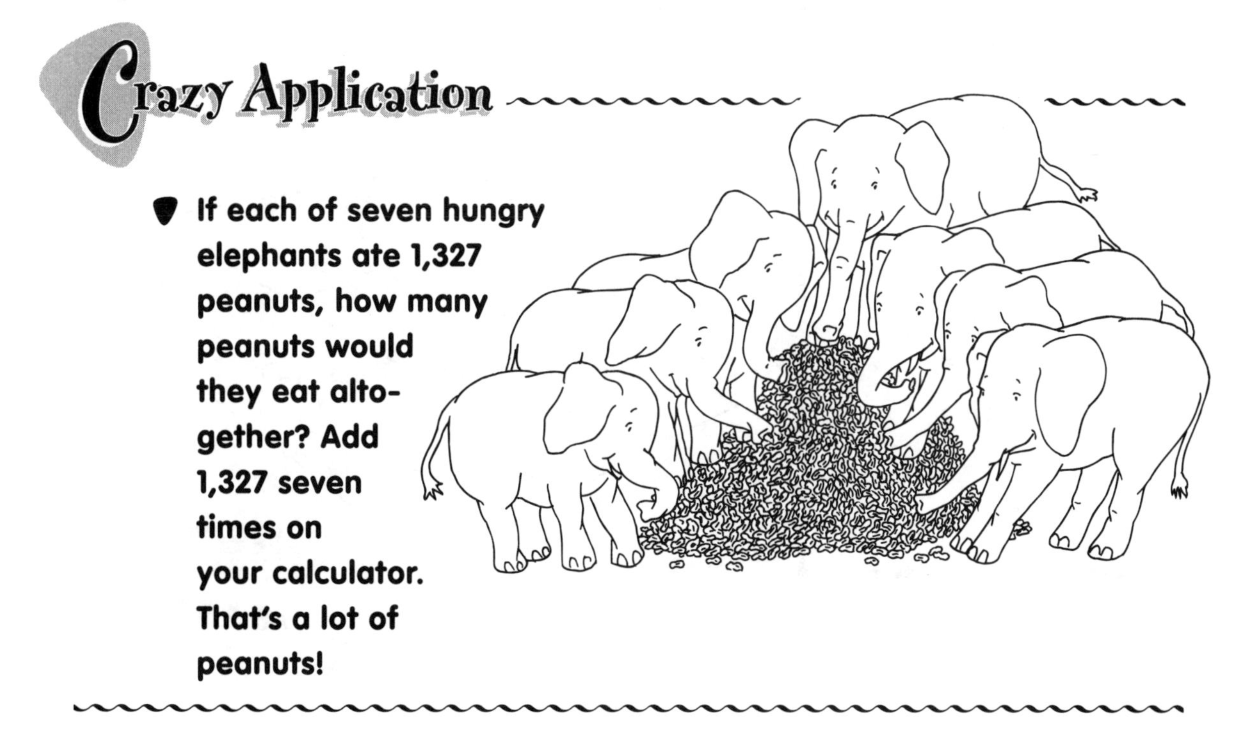

- **If each of seven hungry elephants ate 1,327 peanuts, how many peanuts would they eat altogether? Add 1,327 seven times on your calculator. That's a lot of peanuts!**

Graphing Eights

Use graph paper to learn the 8 times table.

Materials

- pencil
- paper
- graph paper (the larger the squares the better; ¼- or ½-inch graph paper is best)
- crayons

Procedure

1. Write "Eight Times Table" at the top of a piece of paper. Underneath that, write in one column all of the problems that make up the 8 times table, without the answers. Your times table should look like the one here.

Eight Times Table

1 x 8 =

2 x 8 =

3 x 8 =

4 x 8 =

5 x 8 =

6 x 8 =

7 x 8 =

8 x 8 =

9 x 8 =

10 x 8 =

2. On graph paper, use a crayon to draw a rectangle that is one square wide and eight squares long as shown. This rectangle represents the problem 1×8.

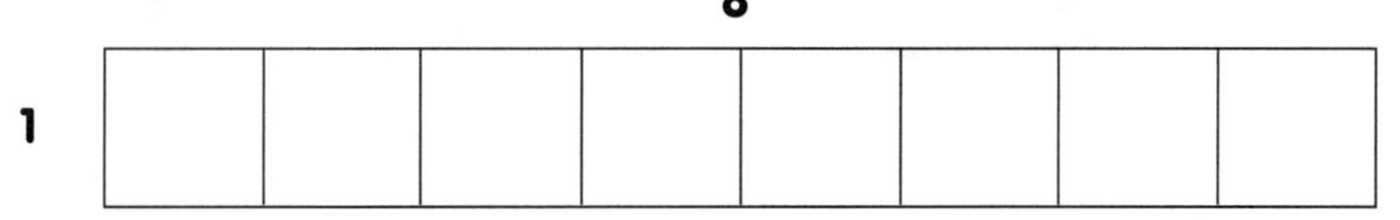

Count the squares that make up this rectangle. There are eight squares, so $1 \times 8 = 8$.

3. To solve the problem 2×8, draw a rectangle two squares wide and eight squares long as shown.

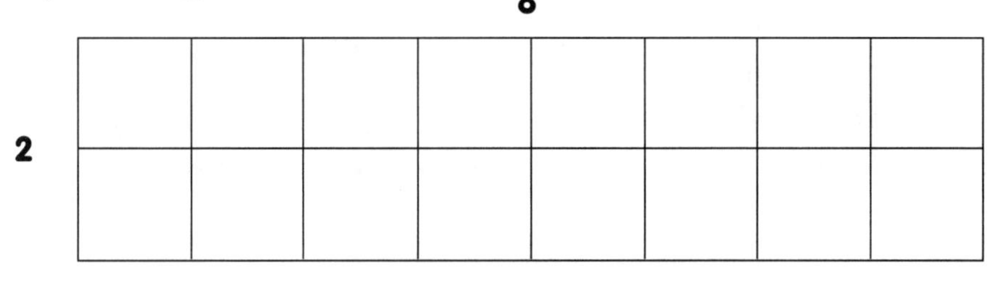

Count the squares that make up this rectangle. There are sixteen squares, so $2 \times 8 = 16$.

4. To solve the problem 3×8, draw a rectangle three squares wide and eight squares long as shown.

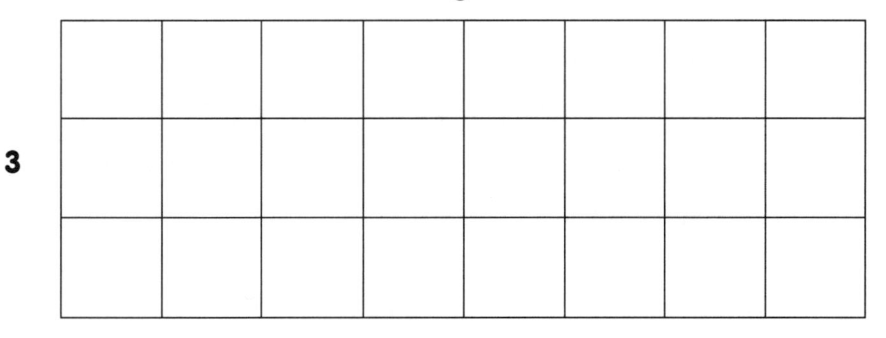

Count the squares that make up this rectangle. There are twenty-four squares, so $3 \times 8 = 24$.

5. Now solve the rest of the problems in the 8 times table using the same method.
6. Fill in the answers in your Eight Times Table. It should now look like the one here.

Eight Times Table
1 x 8 = 8
2 x 8 = 16
3 x 8 = 24
4 x 8 = 32
5 x 8 = 40
6 x 8 = 48
7 x 8 = 56
8 x 8 = 64
9 x 8 = 72
10 x 8 = 80

Practice Makes Perfect

Take three decks of cards and place the ace, two, three, four, five, six, seven, eight, nine, and ten of hearts in a row on the table. Now pull ten eights out of the three decks of cards and place them in a row under the row of hearts. Use this row of eights to help you recite the 8 times table. Point to the ace of hearts and say, "One times eight is eight." Point to the two of hearts and say, "Two times eight is sixteen." Continue for the remaining hearts. If you get stuck on any problem, just count the symbols on as many eights as you're multiplying by.

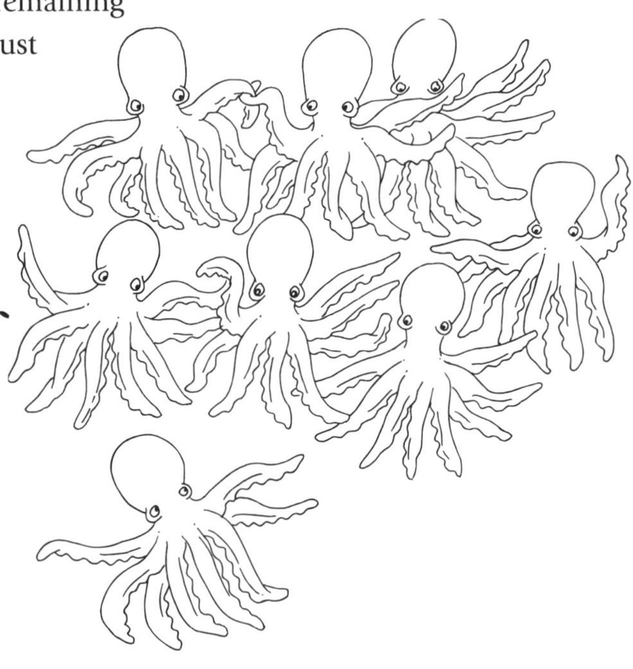

Crazy Application

- **How many arms do eight octopuses have? What is 8 x 8?**

BRAIN Stretcher

You learned 8 x 2 = 16 when you did the "Pair It Up!" activity. Did you notice that two times eight is also sixteen? Draw both of these problems on graph paper. You will notice that even though they look different, they both contain the same number of squares. Turn one of the papers sideways and you will see that the shapes are actually the same.

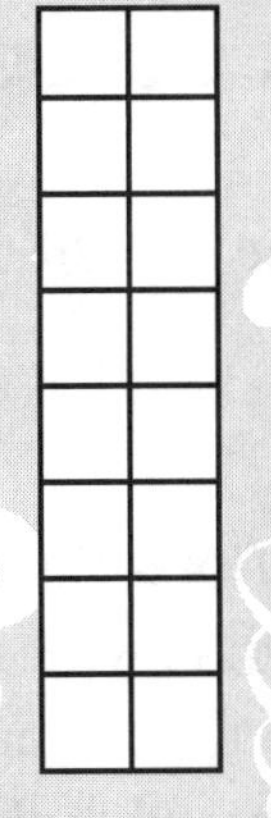

8 x 2 = 16

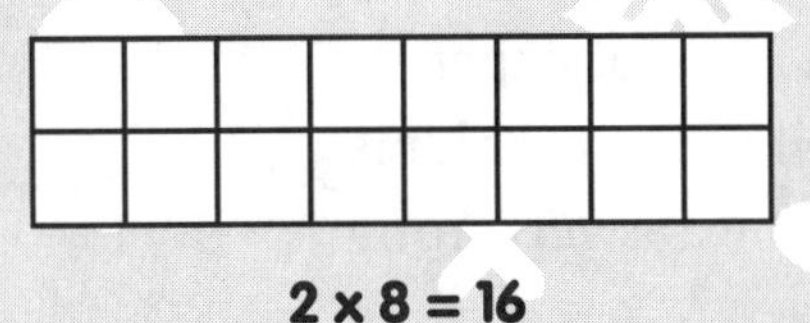

2 x 8 = 16

Try the same thing with 5 x 8 and 8 x 5.

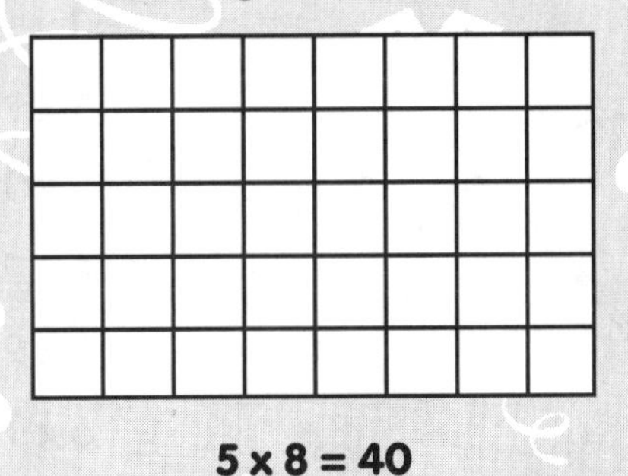

5 x 8 = 40

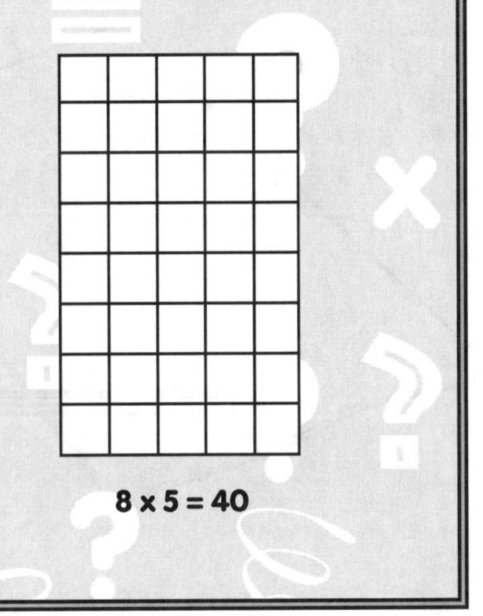

8 x 5 = 40

When you multiply two numbers, the order doesn't matter. You always get the same answer.

Hidden Nines

Find the hidden 9's to learn the 9 times table.

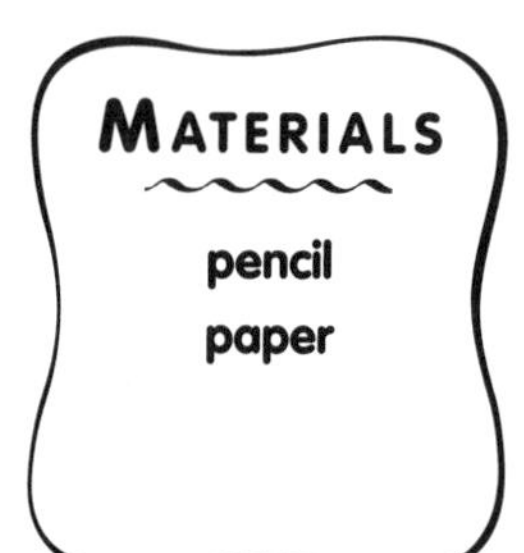

Procedure

1. Write "Nine Times Table" at the top of a piece of paper. Underneath that, write in one column all of the problems that make up the 9 times table, without the answers. Your times table should look like the one here.

Nine Times Table

1 x 9 =

2 x 9 =

3 x 9 =

4 x 9 =

5 x 9 =

6 x 9 =

7 x 9 =

8 x 9 =

9 x 9 =

10 x 9 =

2. Place a 9 in the answer space for the problem 1×9. Why? Since 1×9 is the same as 9×1, we know the answer is 9 just by looking at the 1 times table.
3. Write the numbers 1, 2, 3, 4, 5, 6, 7, 8, and 9 in a column in the answer spaces under the 9 as shown.

1 x 9 = 9
2 x 9 = 1
3 x 9 = 2
4 x 9 = 3
5 x 9 = 4
6 x 9 = 5
7 x 9 = 6
8 x 9 = 7
9 x 9 = 8
10 x 9 = 9

4. Now you're going to learn a little trick to figuring out the 9 times table. A 9 is hidden in each answer, because the digits add up to 9. The first problem now reads $2 \times 9 = 1$. What number should be added to 1 to equal 9? Eight ($1 + 8 = 9$), so place an 8 after the 1. Two times nine is eighteen.
5. The third problem now reads $3 \times 9 = 2$. What number added to 2 will make 9? Seven ($2 + 7 = 9$), so place a 7 after the 2. Three times nine is twenty-seven.
6. Continue finding the hidden 9's to solve the rest of the 9 times table.
7. Fill in the answers in your Nine Times Table. It should now look like the one here.

Nine Times Table

1 x 9 = 9
2 x 9 = 18
3 x 9 = 27
4 x 9 = 36
5 x 9 = 45
6 x 9 = 54
7 x 9 = 63
8 x 9 = 72
9 x 9 = 81
10 x 9 = 90

Practice Makes Perfect

On a piece of paper, write as many pairs of numbers that you can think of that add up to 9. Write them as fast as you can: 18 and 81, 27 and 72, 36 and 63, 45 and 54. Now write the problems that match these answers. Repeat this exercise writing down pairs of numbers that add up to 9 and then writing next to them the multiplication problems that match the answers.

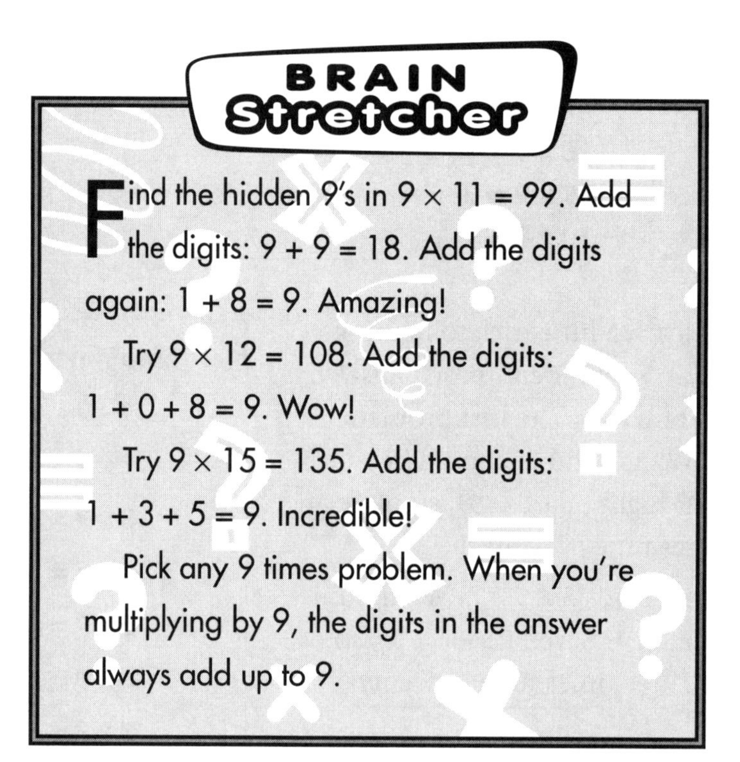

- **If there are nine nectarines in a box, how many nectarines are there in six boxes? What is 6 x 9?**
- **How many players are on eight baseball teams, if there are nine players on each? What is 8 x 9?**

Fingerprints

Learn the 10 times table by counting fingers.

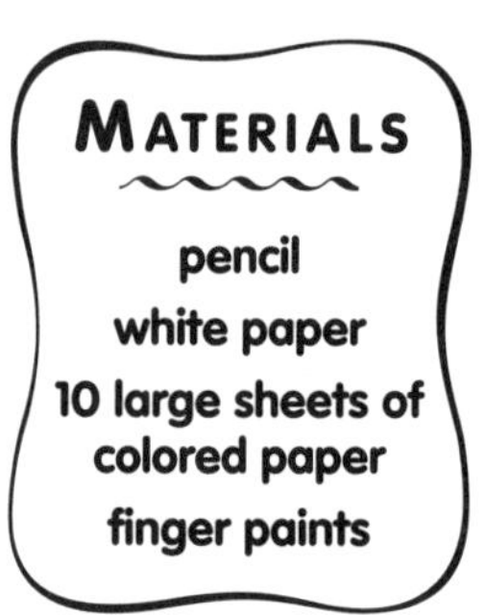

Procedure

1. Write "Ten Times Table" at the top of a piece of paper. Underneath that, write in one column all of the problems that make up the 10 times table, without the answers. Your times table should look like the one here.

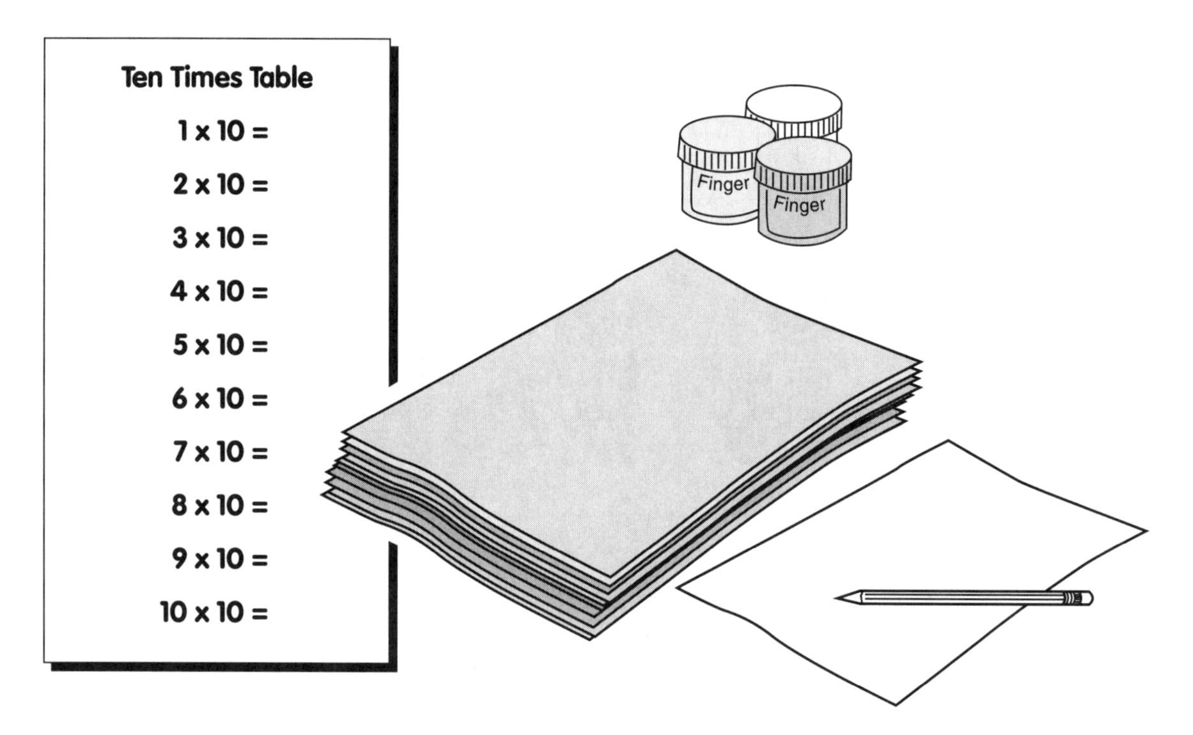

2. At the top of a piece of colored paper, write "1×10." Cover the palms and fingers of both of your hands with finger paint and make handprints of both hands on the colored paper. How many fingerprints did you make? One set of hands is ten fingers, so $1 \times 10 = 10$. 
3. At the top of a second piece of colored paper, write "2×10." Cover both hands with finger paint and make handprints on the paper as before. Wash your hands and use a different color paint to make another set of handprints on the same sheet of paper. How many fingerprints did you make altogether? Two sets of hands is twenty fingers, so $2 \times 10 = 20$. 
4. At the top of a third piece of colored paper, write "3×10." Cover both hands with finger paint and make handprints on the paper as before. Wash your hands and use a different color paint to make another set of handprints on the same sheet of paper. Wash your hands again and use a different color paint to make a third set of handprints on the same sheet of paper. How many fingerprints did you make altogether? Three sets of hands is thirty fingers, so $3 \times 10 = 30$.
5. Continue making handprints to solve the rest of the problems in the 10 times table. Overlap the handprints so they can fit on a single sheet of paper for each problem.

6. Fill in the answers in your Ten Times Table. It should now look like the one here.

Ten Times Table
1 x 10 = 10
2 x 10 = 20
3 x 10 = 30
4 x 10 = 40
5 x 10 = 50
6 x 10 = 60
7 x 10 = 70
8 x 10 = 80
9 x 10 = 90
10 x 10 = 100

Practice Makes Perfect

Use a pile of dimes to practice counting by 10's. Drop the dimes on a table one at a time and count out loud: 10, 20, 30, 40, 50, 60, 70, 80, 90, 100. If you can count by 10's, you know your 10 times table.

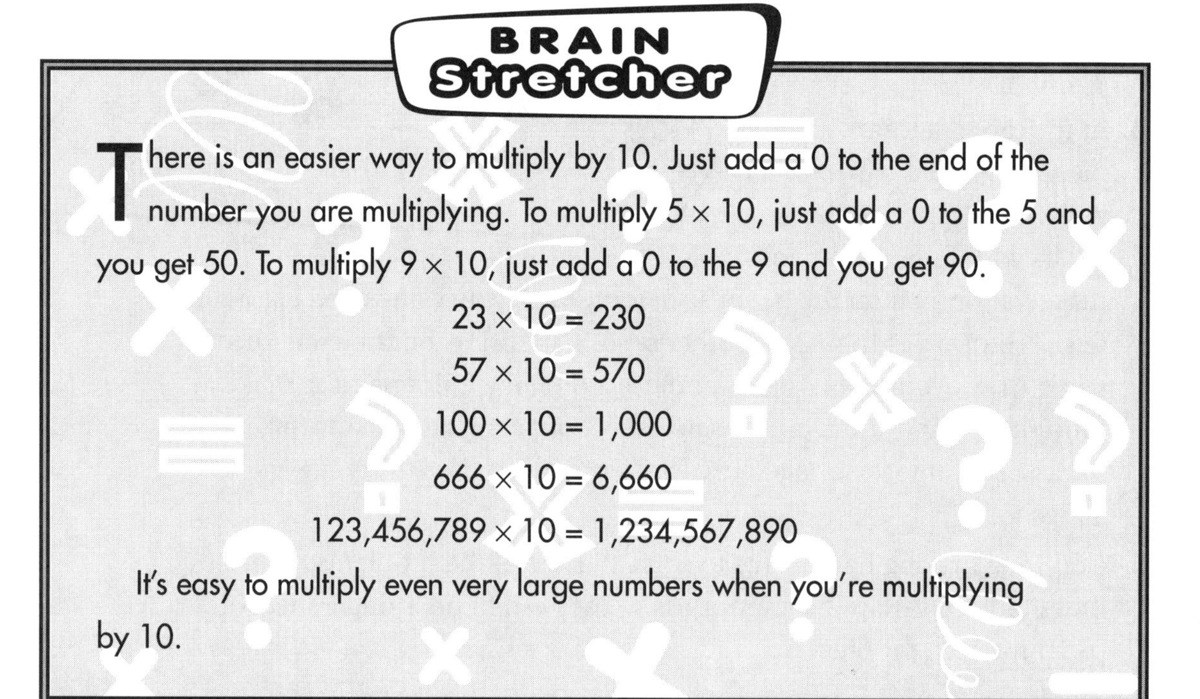

BRAIN Stretcher

There is an easier way to multiply by 10. Just add a 0 to the end of the number you are multiplying. To multiply 5×10, just add a 0 to the 5 and you get 50. To multiply 9×10, just add a 0 to the 9 and you get 90.

$$23 \times 10 = 230$$

$$57 \times 10 = 570$$

$$100 \times 10 = 1{,}000$$

$$666 \times 10 = 6{,}660$$

$$123{,}456{,}789 \times 10 = 1{,}234{,}567{,}890$$

It's easy to multiply even very large numbers when you're multiplying by 10.

To multiply any number by 100, just add two 0's. To find 5×100, add two 0's to 5: $5 \times 100 = 500$. What is 123×100? Just add two 0's to 123 and you get 12,300.

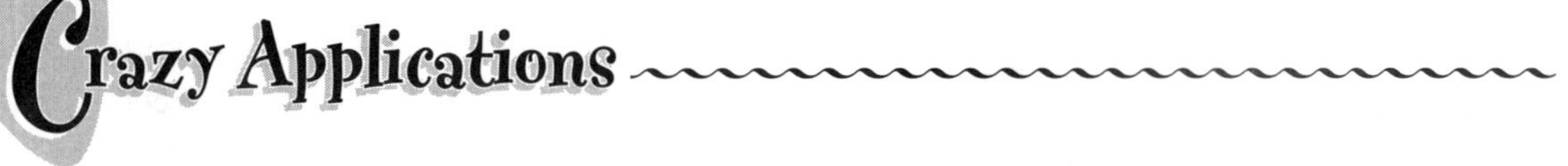

- **How many toe prints would a family of five make? What is 5 x 10?**
- **How many toes does a soccer team have? What is 11 x 10?**
- **How many bowling pins in a hundred ten-pin bowling lanes? What is 100 x 10? Whether you add one 0 to 100 or two 0's to 10, you get the same answer: 1,000!**

Big Fat Zero

Try this to learn what happens when you multiply by 0.

MATERIALS

marker
paper

Procedure

Use the marker to draw a giant 0 on a piece of paper. Now you know the answer to every problem in the 0 times table! When you multiply any number by 0 or 0 by any number, the answer is always 0.

$1 \times 0 = 0.$
$5 \times 0 = 0.$
$100 \times 0 = 0.$
$1{,}000 \times 0 = 0.$
$1{,}000{,}000 \times 0 = 0.$
$0 \times 0 =$ guess what?
You've got it: 0.

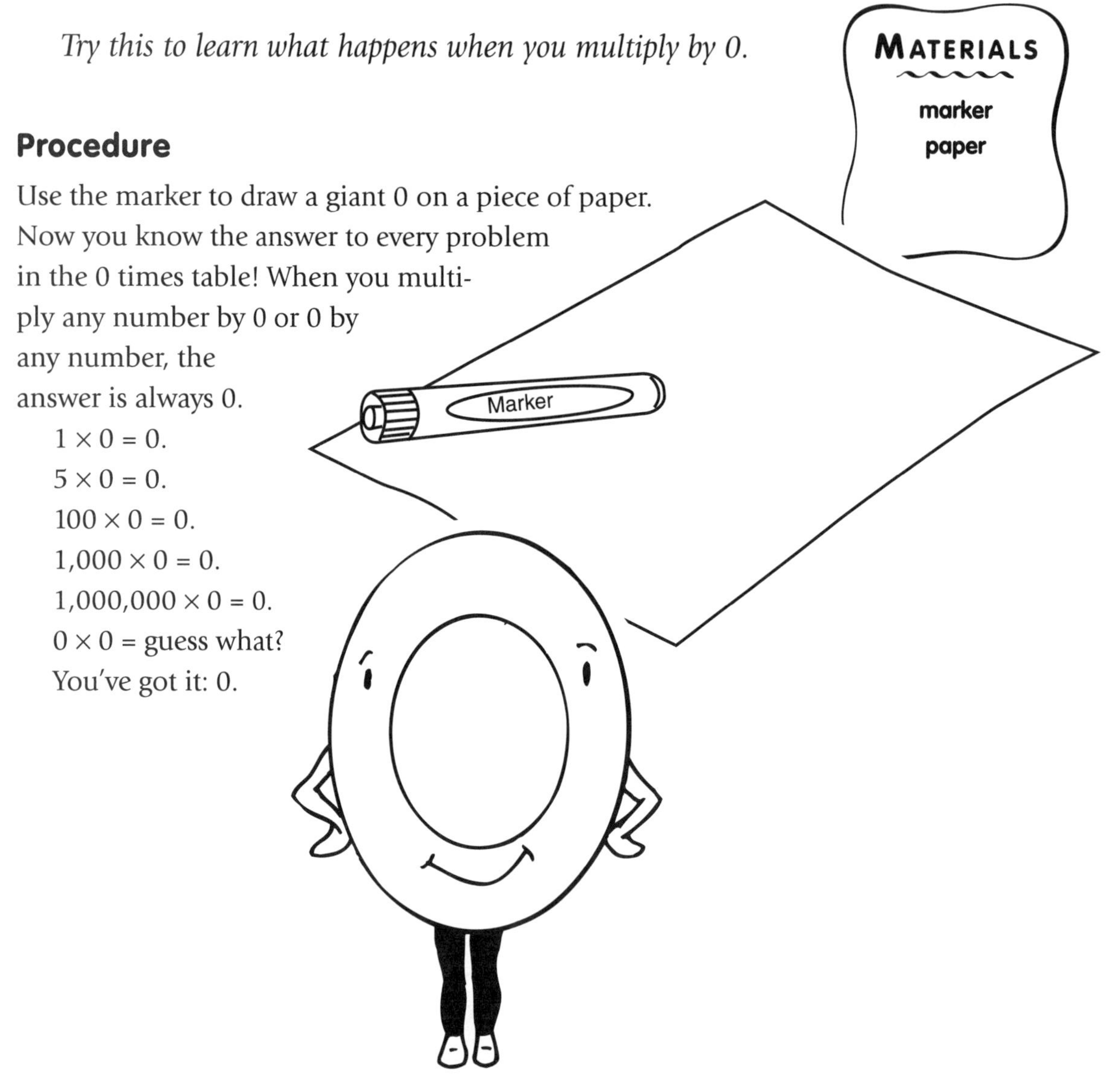

BRAIN Stretcher

When you multiply two numbers together and the answer is 0, what can you say about the two numbers? Any clue?

If mystery number 1 times mystery number 2 equals 0, then either mystery number 1 is 0 or mystery number 2 is 0 or both mystery numbers 1 and 2 are 0.

- **If you deposit $0 in the bank every day for the next 10 years, how much money will you have saved? What is 365 x 10 x 0?**

Book It!

Now that you have successfully figured out all of the multiplication tables, what can you do with them? How about putting them all together in a book?

Materials

- 2 pieces of colored construction paper
- crayons or colored pencils
- magazines
- glue
- stapler

Procedure

1. Take a piece of colored construction paper and make a front cover for your book. Decorate the cover with crayons, magazine clippings, or anything else you like. Write the title of your book in the middle of the cover: "(Your name's) Multiplication Tables Book." If you have a computer, you could use computer graphics on your cover.
2. When you are done, put your ten multiplication tables in order. Put your cover on top and put the other blank piece of construction paper on the bottom of the stack.
3. Staple all of the pages together along the left side.
4. Use your book to study and practice the multiplication tables.

III

Multiplication Practice Games

Now that you know your multiplication tables, it's time for some fast and furious practice. It's easy to understand the multiplication tables one at a time, but what happens when the problems are all mixed together? Frequent practice will help you recall each of the one hundred multiplication facts faster. It is important that you know the multiplication tables as well as you know your name.

Practice does not have to be boring or feel like work. Instead it can be fun and exciting. This section contains games to help you practice the multiplication tables. With enough practice, you'll become a multiplication whiz!

Cover-Up!

Play a dice game with a friend to practice the multiplication tables from 1 to 6.

Materials

pencil
paper
dice
poker chips or pennies
2 players

Game Preparation

Use pencil and paper to make a game card for each player. The game card should look like a bingo card and contain the numbers from 1 to 36. The game card should have six rows and six columns as shown.

Game Rules

1. Players take turns rolling the dice.
2. After each player rolls the dice, he or she multiplies the two numbers faceup on the dice. This number is the product.
   The player then puts a poker chip on the number on his game card that matches the product. If that number is already covered, the player does not cover any number.

Cover-Up!

1	2	3	4	5	6
7	8	9	10	11	12
13	14	15	16	17	18
19	20	21	22	23	24
25	26	27	28	29	30
31	32	33	34	35	36

3. Doubles are wild. A player who rolls doubles can cover any number on his or her game card. That player also gets another turn.
4. The first player to cover his or her entire game card is the winner.
5. For a shorter version of Cover-Up! the first player who covers six in a row, either horizontally, vertically, or diagonally, wins the game.

SUPER COVER-UP!

1. Make a new game card with the numbers from 1 to 25. Your new game card should have five rows and five columns as shown.

1	2	3	4	5
6	7	8	9	10
11	12	13	14	15
16	17	18	19	20
21	22	23	24	25

2. Now cover the number 2 and all the multiples of 2, and notice the pattern formed. How does the pattern on this game card differ from the pattern formed when you covered these numbers on the other game card? Why is there a difference?
3. Now cover 3 and all the multiples of 3, and notice the pattern formed. How does this pattern differ from the pattern formed when you covered these numbers on the other game card? Why is there a difference?
4. Now cover 4 and all the multiples of 4, and notice the pattern formed. How does this pattern differ from the pattern formed when you covered these numbers on the other game? Why is there a difference?
5. Can you predict how the patterns would change if you changed the number of rows and columns? How would the patterns change if the game card had only four rows and columns and you covered the same numbers?

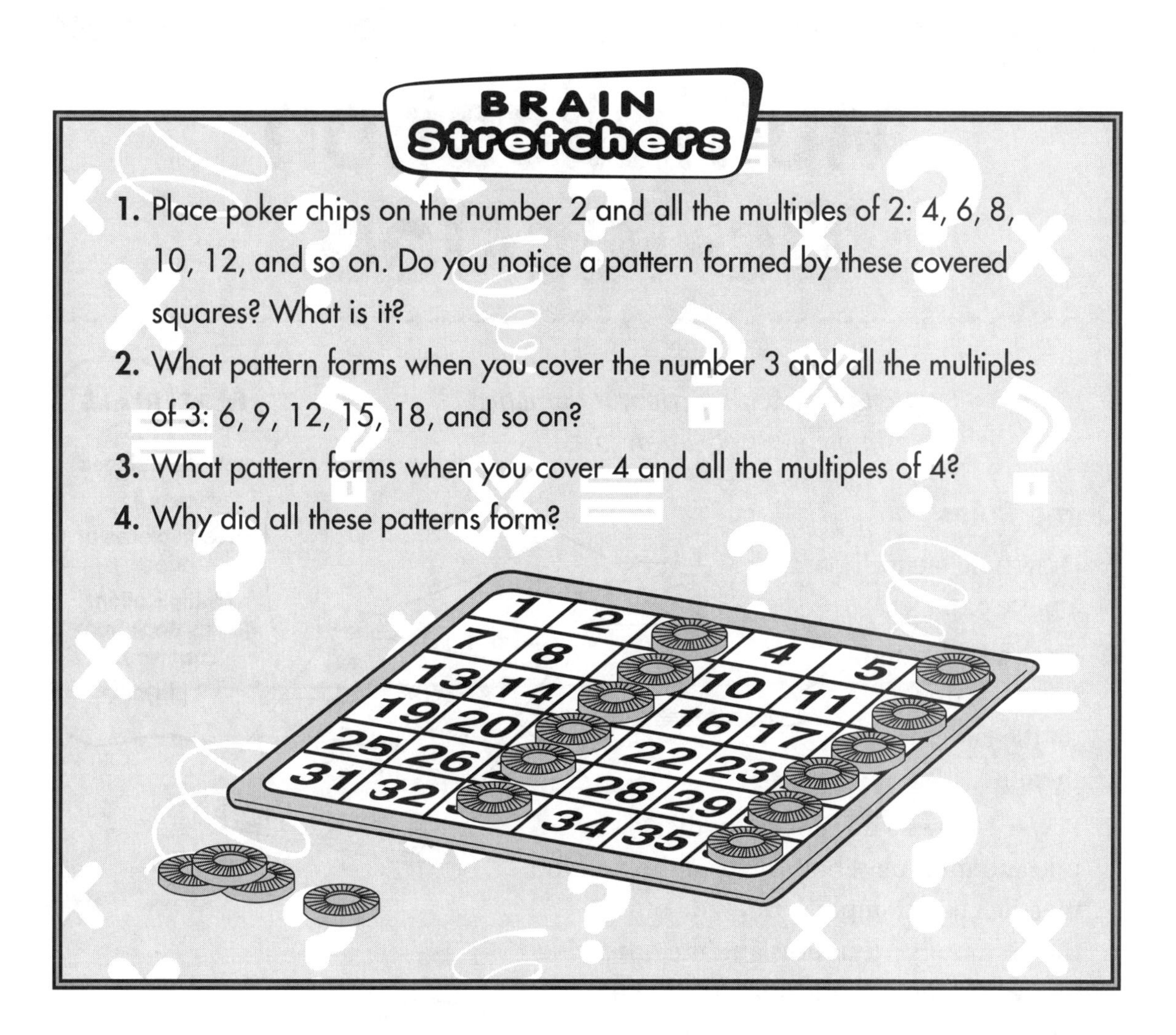

BRAIN Stretchers

1. Place poker chips on the number 2 and all the multiples of 2: 4, 6, 8, 10, 12, and so on. Do you notice a pattern formed by these covered squares? What is it?
2. What pattern forms when you cover the number 3 and all the multiples of 3: 6, 9, 12, 15, 18, and so on?
3. What pattern forms when you cover 4 and all the multiples of 4?
4. Why did all these patterns form?

14

Multiplication Tic-Tac-Toe

Play tic-tac-toe with a friend to practice simple multiplication facts.

MATERIALS

- set of dominoes
- pencil
- several pieces of paper
- Multiplication Tables Book from chapter 12
- 2 players

Game Rules

1. Draw a tic-tac-toe board on a piece of paper.
2. Place all the dominoes face-down on the table. Mix them up. 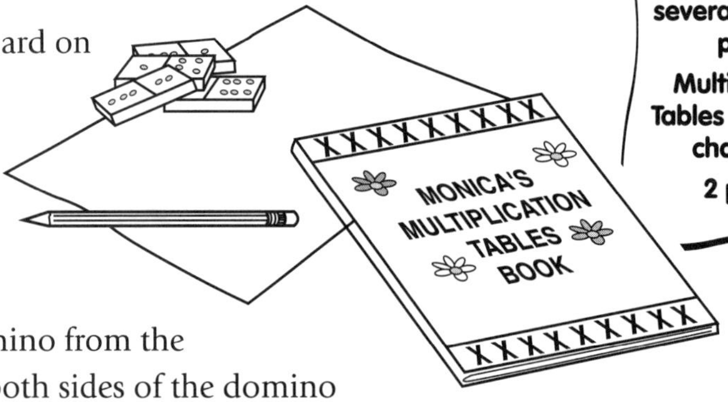
3. Player 1 draws a domino from the pile and multiplies both sides of the domino together. For example, if one side of the domino has four dots and the other side of the domino has one dot, then the problem is 4×1 and the correct answer is 4. If player 1 solves the problem correctly by saying, "Four," he or she can place an X anywhere on the tic-tac-toe board. But if player 1 solves the problem incorrectly, he or she loses that turn. Check the answers in your Multiplication Tables Book if there's any question.

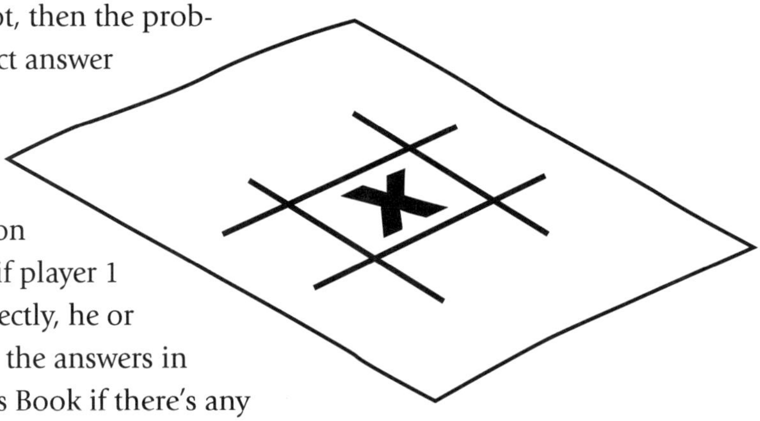

4. Player 2 then draws a domino from the pile and multiplies both sides of the domino together. If the player solves the problem correctly, he or she can place an O in any remaining space on the board. But if the player solves the problem incorrectly, he or she loses that turn.
5. The game continues until one player wins by getting three X's or O's in a row, or no one gets three in a row and all the squares are filled.
6. Start another multiplication tic-tac-toe game, using the same rules. When there are no dominoes left, the player who has won the most games is the winner.

SUPER MULTIPLICATION TIC-TAC-TOE

Each player draws two dominoes at a time and multiplies all four numbers without the benefit of paper or pencil. If a player solves the problem correctly, he or she can place an X or an O in any empty space on the tic-tac-toe board.

Fingers!

Play this fast-paced multiplication drill with a friend to help you learn the multiplication tables from 0 to 5.

Materials

2 players

Game Rules

1. Two players stand facing each other, each holding one hand behind his or her back.
2. Player 1 calls out, "Ready, set, fingers!" At the call of "Fingers!" both players put out their hidden hands and show either zero, one, two, three, four, or five fingers.
3. Both players multiply the number of fingers on both hands. The first player to call out the correct answer wins an *F*, the first letter in the word *FINGERS*.
4. Both players again hide one hand and player 2 calls out, "Ready, set, fingers!" At the call of "Fingers!" both players show zero to five fingers.

5. Both players multiply the number of fingers on both hands. The first player to call out the correct answer wins the next letter in the word *FINGERS*.
6. Play continues in the same manner until one of the players wins all the letters.

SUPER FINGERS!

Once you've mastered Fingers! try Super Fingers! Super Fingers! is played exactly like Fingers! except players use the fingers of both hands, so they have the choice of showing zero to ten fingers. This will help you practice all of the multiplication tables.

SUPER DISAPPEARING FINGERS!

If you think you've mastered Super Fingers!, try Super Disappearing Fingers! When you play Super Disappearing Fingers! a player who calls out a wrong answer loses a letter.

Possible or Impossible

Practice the multiplication tables by creating problems from random numbers.

MATERIALS

pencil
2 index cards
4 dice
2 or more players

Game Preparation

Write a multiplication sign (×) on one index card. Write an equals sign (=) on the other index card.

Game Rules

1. Players take turns saying either "Possible" or "Impossible," then rolling the four dice.
2. Using the numbers rolled and the index cards, the player tries to make a true problem. For example, if the player rolled 1, 2, 2, 6, he or she could make either of the following true problems: $2 \times 6 = 12$ or $1 \times 2 = 2$. Notice that $1 \times 2 = 2$ does not use all the numbers rolled. That is okay. If the player guessed possible, he or she earns 1 point. But if the player guessed impossible, he or she loses that turn. If the player rolled 1, 2, 3, 5, he or she could not make a true problem with any of the numbers. If the player guessed impossible, he or she earns 1 point. But if the player guessed possible, he or she loses that turn.
3. The first player to earn 5 points wins the game. Points are earned based on whether the player guessed correctly, not whether a true problem was created.

Shout It Out!

Play this fun game using cards and one die to practice the multiplication tables from 1 to 6.

Game Preparation

Remove all the face cards (kings, queens, jacks) and jokers from a deck of playing cards. There should be forty cards left.

Game Rules

1. Shuffle the cards and place them facedown in a stack in the center of the table.
2. Player 1 rolls the die. Whatever number is rolled is the multiplier. The players will multiply the numbers on each card played by this multiplier. For example, if a 2 is rolled, the value of the card will be multiplied by 2.
3. Player 1 turns over the top card on the stack. Each player multiplies the value of the card by the multiplier. The first player to shout out the correct answer wins the card.

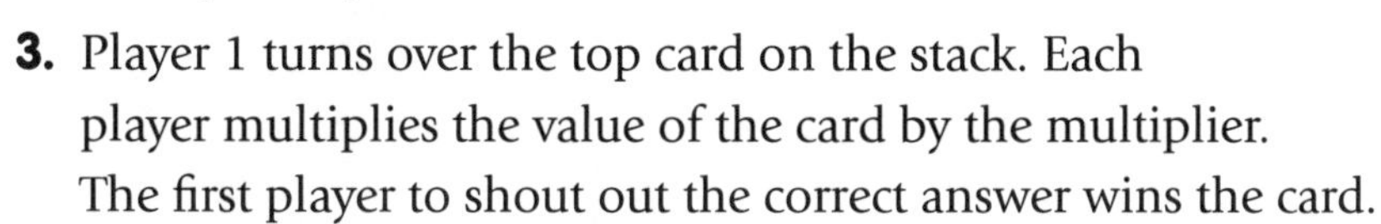

4. If two or more players shout out the answer at the same time, the card is placed at the bottom of the pile.
5. If one player thinks another player shouted out an incorrect answer, the challenging player shouts, "Challenge!" and the answer is checked on a calculator. If the answer was incorrect, the challenging player wins the card. But if the answer was correct, the challenged player takes another card off the top of the stack and adds it to his or her winnings pile.
6. Player 2 turns the next card over and play continues as before. The players now multiply the value of this card by the same multiplier.
7. When all of the cards in the stack are gone, the round is over. The player with the most cards wins the round.
8. For each new round, shuffle all of the cards again and place them face-down in the center of the table. Let another player roll the die to get a new multiplier. The first player to win three rounds wins the game.

SUPER SHOUT IT OUT!

If you want more advanced multiplication practice, roll two dice instead of one. Multiply the value of each card by the total on both dice. Playing with two dice will give you practice with the multiplication tables from 2 to 12.

18

Split Second

Work against the clock to solve the multiplication tables.

Materials

pencil
several pieces of paper
dice
timer or clock with second hand
2 players

Game Rules

1. On a piece of paper, player 2 writes down five problems from the multiplication tables for player 1 to solve. The problems should be a one-digit number times a one-digit number, such as 5×2 or 8×4.
2. Player 1 rolls the dice and multiplies the numbers rolled to determine how many seconds he or she has to answer all of the problems.
3. Player 2 places the problems facedown in front of player 1. When player 1 turns the problems faceup, player 2 starts the timer. Player 1 solves as many of the problems as he or she can before the time is up and player 2 shouts, "Stop!" Player 1 earns 1 point for each problem solved correctly.

4. The players switch roles and play again.
5. The first player to earn 21 points wins the game.

SUPER SPLIT SECOND

Once you get good at playing Split Second, you can play Super Split Second using more complicated multiplication problems. The rules are the same as for Split Second, but now all the problems should be a two-digit number times a one-digit number, such as 24×2, 38×9, or 17×6. Super Split Second is a lot harder than Split Second because you'll probably never have enough time to solve all of the problems.

19 Multiplication Search

Challenge a friend to find multiplication problems and their answers in a number puzzle.

Materials

pencil
several pieces of graph paper
2 or more players

Game Rules

1. Each player marks off an area that is seven squares by seven squares on his or her piece of graph paper.
2. In these forty-nine squares, each player makes a number puzzle by hiding ten multiplication problems and their answers. The problems can be hidden horizontally or vertically. The problems should be a one-digit number times a one-digit number. If the answer is a two-digit number, it should be split up into two adjacent squares. Fill in the unused spaces with random numbers.
3. The players switch puzzles. The first player to find all ten hidden problems is the winner.

Here is a sample Multiplication Search puzzle. Ten problems and their answers are hidden. Can you find them?

2	3	6	9	9	8	1
9	1	5	6	0	2	0
5	3	3	7	5	5	2
5	5	0	5	3	8	7
1	5	4	8	3	2	1
5	7	4	6	9	2	4
9	2	3	7	7	4	9

Look in the first row at the first three numbers: 2, 3, 6. You have found the first hidden multiplication problem: $2 \times 3 = 6$

2	3	6	9	9	8	1
9	1	5	6	0	2	0
5	3	3	7	5	5	2
5	5	0	5	3	8	7
1	5	4	8	3	2	1
5	7	4	6	9	2	4
9	2	3	7	7	4	9

2	3	6	9	9	8	1
9	1	5	6	0	2	0
5	3	3	7	5	5	2
5	5	0	5	3	8	7
1	5	4	8	3	2	1
5	7	4	6	9	2	4
9	2	3	7	7	4	9

Now look in the third column at the first four numbers: 6, 5, 3, 0. This is the second hidden problem: $6 \times 5 = 30$.

Now find the other eight hidden problems.

SUPER MULTIPLICATION SEARCH

If you want to make the game more challenging, hide problems that are a two-digit number times a one-digit number. Just make sure the product is less than 100. Sample problems are 42×2, 31×3, 12×7, 21×4.

Off to the Races

Compete with your family and friends to see who can say the multiplication tables the fastest.

Game Preparation

At the top of a blackboard, write "Record Holders." Down the left-hand side of the board, write the names of the multiplication tables as shown.

Record Holders

1 x
2 x
3 x
4 x
5 x
6 x
7 x
8 x
9 x
10 x

Game Rules

1. Player 1 chooses a multiplication table to recite. Player 2 times how fast the first player recites the entire multiplication table.
2. Player 1 starts out as the record holder. His or her name and time are recorded on the Record Holders board next to the multiplication table chosen.
3. The other players in turn each recite a multiplication table. It can be the same table or a different one.
4. Any time a player sets a new record, the new record is written on the Record Holders board. Previous records are crossed out or erased.
5. The game can continue forever. Players can play any time they have a few extra minutes to try to beat the existing records. Keep the Record Holders board posted at all times.

SUPER OFF TO THE RACES

Add the 11 and 12 times tables to your Record Holders board. See how fast these tables can be recited.

OFF TO THE RACES SOLITAIRE

If you can't find a friend to practice with, compete against yourself. Write your times on the Record Holders board. Keep practicing and as your times improve, erase your old times and put your new times on the board.

21 Multiplication Crossword Puzzle

Practice your multiplication tables while creating a crossword puzzle.

MATERIALS

pencil
paper

Procedure

Design a crossword puzzle of number problems using a blank grid like the one shown. Fill in the problems and the answers. Make sure the answers fit in the one- or two-digit spaces provided. Here are a few problems and answers to get you started.

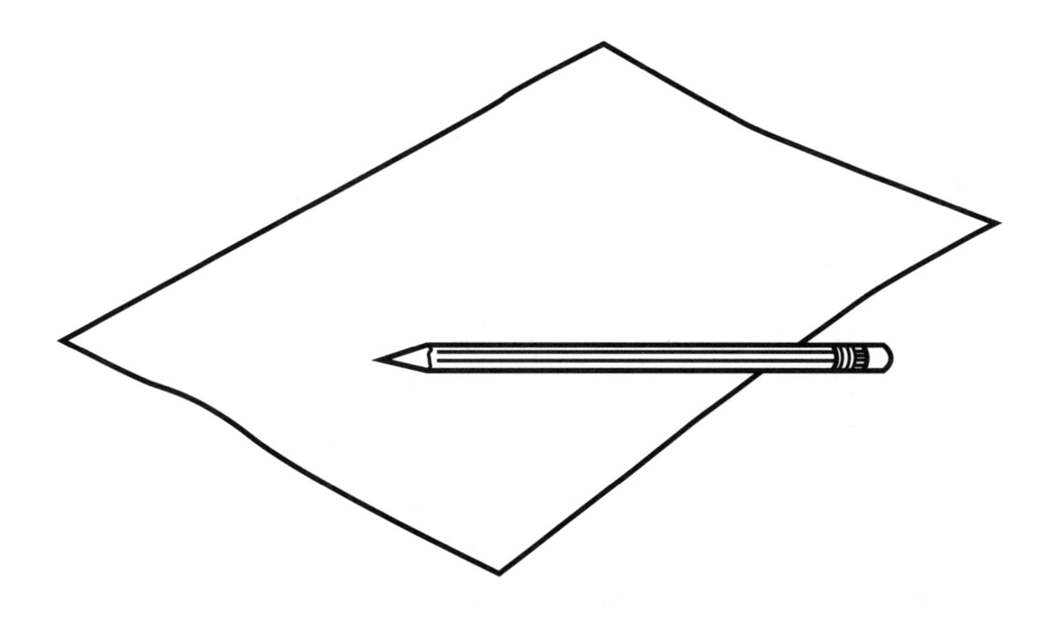

1. 2	4		2. 3	5		3.	
1		4. 4	0		5.		
	6.			7.			8.
9.			10.			11.	
		12.			13.		
	14.			15.			16.

Across

1. 6×4
2. 7×5
3.
4. 8×5
5.
6.
7.
8.
9.
10.
11.
12.
13.
14.
15.
16.

Down

1. 7×3
2. 10×3
3.
4.
5.
6.
7.
8.
9.
10.
11.
12.
13.
14.
15.
16.

Notice 1 across is 6×4, which is 24, and 1 down is 7×3, which is 21. Both of these answers share the 2 in the top left square of the crossword puzzle.

22 Multiplication War

Play a fast-paced multiplication card game for two players based on the game of war.

MATERIALS

playing cards
2 players

Game Preparation

Remove the face cards (kings, queens, jacks) and jokers from a deck of playing cards. There should be forty cards left.

Game Rules

1. Each player is dealt twenty cards. Both players place their cards facedown in a stack in front of them.
2. The players turn their top card over at the same time and multiply the values of the two cards. The first player to shout out the correct answer wins both cards.
3. If both players shout out the correct answer at exactly the same time, you have a multiplication war! Both players together place three new cards facedown and a fourth new card faceup in front of

them. The first player to shout out the correct product of the two faceup cards wins all eight cards plus the two played before the war—ten cards altogether.

4. If either player shouts out a wrong answer, the other player wins both cards or, in the case of a war, all ten cards.
5. The game continues until one player wins all the cards.

MULTIPLICATION WAR SOLITAIRE

If you don't have a friend to play with, you can practice your multiplication tables by yourself with a deck of playing cards and a calculator.

1. Take out all the face cards (kings, queens, jacks) and jokers.
2. Shuffle the cards and place the deck facedown in front of you. Turn the top two cards over and multiply their values. If you can multiply them quickly, put them facedown on your left. If you cannot, put them facedown in a pile on your right.
3. Continue multiplying the values of pairs of cards until you have gone through the entire deck.
4. How many values did you multiply quickly? Check your answers on the calculator.
5. Shuffle the cards and try again. See if you can beat your old score.

Unscramble

Practice all the multiplication tables by solving scrambled problems.

Game Preparation

Write one of the following multiplication problems on each of one hundred index cards:

1 x 1	1 x 2	1 x 3	1 x 4	1 x 5	1 x 6	1 x 7	1 x 8	1 x 9	1 x 10
2 x 1	2 x 2	2 x 3	2 x 4	2 x 5	2 x 6	2 x 7	2 x 8	2 x 9	2 x 10
3 x 1	3 x 2	3 x 3	3 x 4	3 x 5	3 x 6	3 x 7	3 x 8	3 x 9	3 x 10
4 x 1	4 x 2	4 x 3	4 x 4	4 x 5	4 x 6	4 x 7	4 x 8	4 x 9	4 x 10
5 x 1	5 x 2	5 x 3	5 x 4	5 x 5	5 x 6	5 x 7	5 x 8	5 x 9	5 x 10
6 x 1	6 x 2	6 x 3	6 x 4	6 x 5	6 x 6	6 x 7	6 x 8	6 x 9	6 x 10
7 x 1	7 x 2	7 x 3	7 x 4	7 x 5	7 x 6	7 x 7	7 x 8	7 x 9	7 x 10
8 x 1	8 x 2	8 x 3	8 x 4	8 x 5	8 x 6	8 x 7	8 x 8	8 x 9	8 x 10
9 x 1	9 x 2	9 x 3	9 x 4	9 x 5	9 x 6	9 x 7	9 x 8	9 x 9	9 x 10
10 x 1	10 x 2	10 x 3	10 x 4	10 x 5	10 x 6	10 x 7	10 x 8	10 x 9	10 x 10

Game Rules

1. Shuffle the cards and deal each player ten cards. The players place their ten cards facedown in a pile in front of them.
2. One player shouts "Unscramble!" and each player turns all of his or her cards over and places them in a row. Players rearrange their cards in order from lowest to highest answer by solving the problems on the cards. For example, say the following cards are turned over:

6×2 4×2 8×3 5×7 5×1 9×7 2×9 3×3 8×6 5×5

The player would have to rearrange them in the following order:

5×1 4×2 3×3 6×2 2×9 8×3 5×5 5×7 8×6 9×7

The answers to these problems are now in numerical order:

5 8 9 12 18 24 25 35 48 63

3. The first player to put his or her cards in order wins the round.
4. Shuffle the remaining cards and play again. The first player to win two rounds wins the game.

UNSCRAMBLE SOLITAIRE

If you don't have a friend to play with, you can play Unscramble by yourself. Shuffle the cards and deal yourself the top ten cards. Time how long it takes you to put these ten cards in order from lowest to highest answer. Record your time. Now take the next ten cards and see how long it takes you to put them in order. Did you beat your last score?

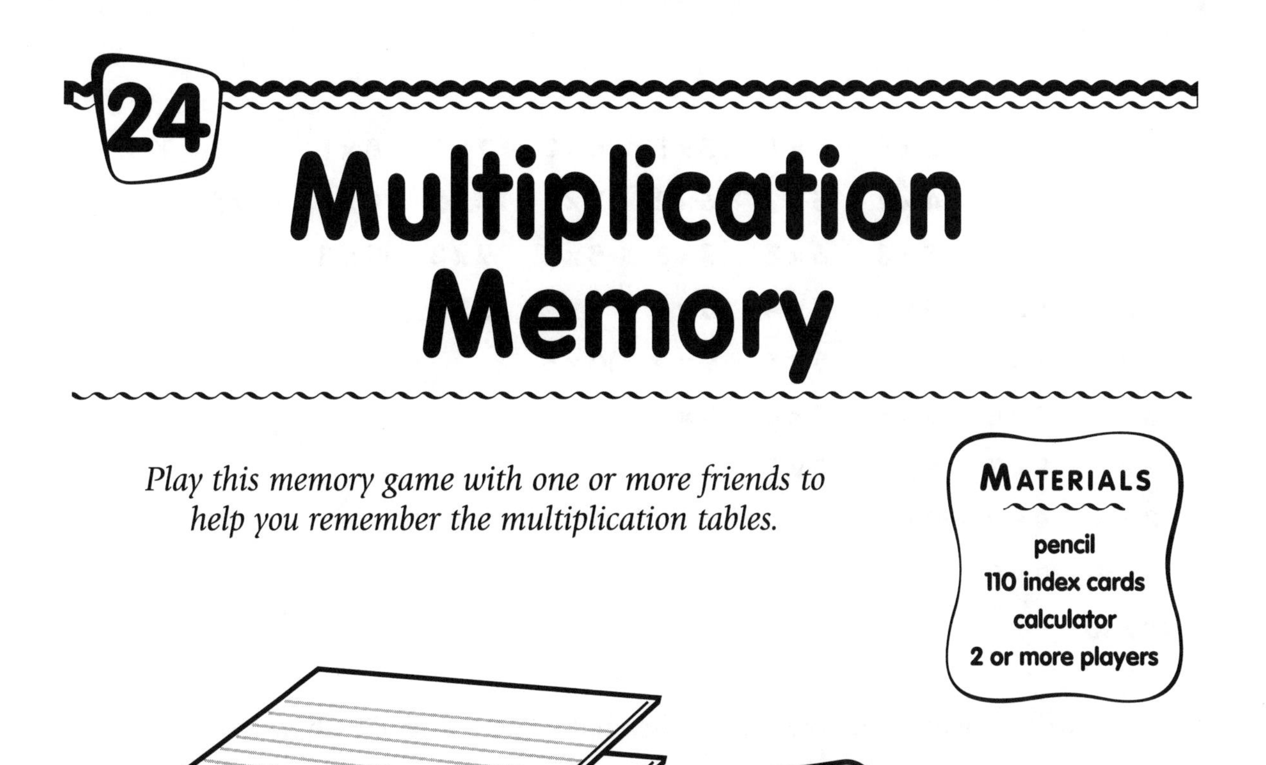

24 Multiplication Memory

Play this memory game with one or more friends to help you remember the multiplication tables.

MATERIALS

pencil
110 index cards
calculator
2 or more players

Game Preparation

1. Take fifty-five index cards and write "MP" on one side of each. MP stands for multiplication problem. It tells you that the card has a multiplication problem on the other side.
2. Take another fifty-five index cards and write "A" on one side of each. A stands for answer. It tells you that the card has an answer on the other side.
3. On the blank side of each MP card, write one of the following multiplication problems.

1 x 1	2 x 1	3 x 1	4 x 1	5 x 1	6 x 1	7 x 1	8 x 1	9 x 1	10 x 1
2 x 2	3 x 2	4 x 2	5 x 2	6 x 2	7 x 2	8 x 2	9 x 2	10 x 2	
3 x 3	4 x 3	5 x 3	6 x 3	7 x 3	8 x 3	9 x 3	10 x 3		
4 x 4	5 x 4	6 x 4	7 x 4	8 x 4	9 x 4	10 x 4			
5 x 5	6 x 5	7 x 5	8 x 5	9 x 5	10 x 5				
6 x 6	7 x 6	8 x 6	9 x 6	10 x 6					
7 x 7	8 x 7	9 x 7	10 x 7						
8 x 8	9 x 8	10 x 8							
9 x 9	10 x 9								
10 x 10									

4. Now write one of the following answers on the blank side of each A card.

1	2	3	4	5	6	7	8	9	10
4	6	8	10	12	14	16	18	20	
9	12	15	18	21	24	27	30		
16	20	24	28	32	36	40			
25	30	35	40	45	50				
36	42	48	54	60					
49	56	63	70						
64	72	80							
81	90								
100									

5. Keep the MP cards and the A cards in two separate piles.

Game Rules

1. Shuffle the MP cards. Place them on the table in five rows, eleven cards per row, so that the problem side of each card is facedown.
2. Shuffle the A cards. Place them in another area of the table in five rows so that the answer side of each card is facedown.
3. Players take turns turning over two cards, one MP card and one A card. If the card with the problem matches the card with the answer (cards match when the answer is correct), the player keeps the pair of cards and takes another turn. If the cards do not match (the answer is not a correct solution), then the cards are returned facedown to their original places and the next player takes a turn. (Use a calculator to check the answers to problems you're not sure about.)
4. Play continues until there are no cards left. The player with the most cards wins.

25

Silly Multiple Stories

Write a silly story using the multiples of a number.

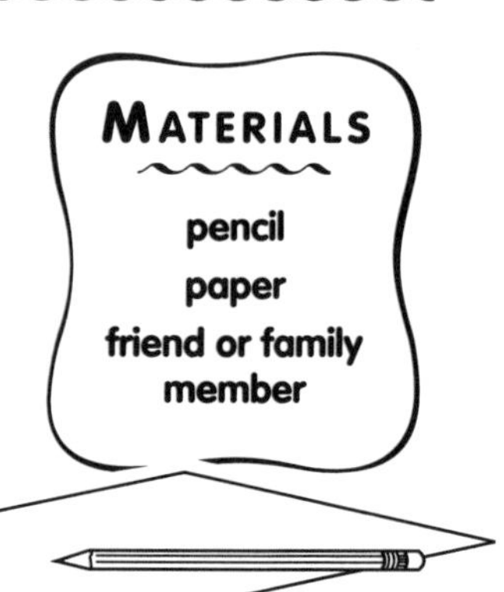

Procedure

1. Write a silly story using the multiples of a specific number in order. For example, if you use all the multiples of the number 4, your story would include the numbers 4, 8, 12, 16, 20, 24, 28, 32, 36, and 40.
2. Read your story to a friend or family member and ask, "Is there anything unusual about this story?" Or you and a friend could both write silly multiple stories and see whose story is the silliest.
3. After you have written your story, draw a picture of it. For example:

"Three"

The Zoo family had three children. Jason, age 6; Caryn, age 9; and Nicole, age 12. They lived at 15 South Eighteenth Street. Jason loved dogs and owned twenty-one Yorkshire terriers. Caryn loved cats and owned twenty-four Siamese cats. Nicole, a bird lover, owned twenty-seven canaries. Yesterday, June 30, was just an ordinary day. The children spent the entire day cleaning up after their pets and watching Jason's dogs chase Caryn's cats, which were chasing Nicole's birds.

Multiple Search

Practice the multiplication table of any number while you draw a hidden picture.

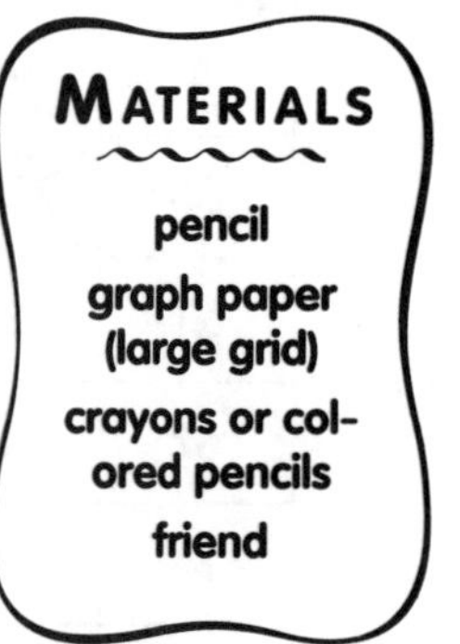

Procedure

1. With a pencil, mark an area eight squares long and eight squares wide on graph paper.
2. Pick a number from 2 to 12 and write the multiples of that number in some of the empty squares so that they form a pattern or picture.
3. Fill in the remaining squares with random numbers that are not multiples of the number you selected.

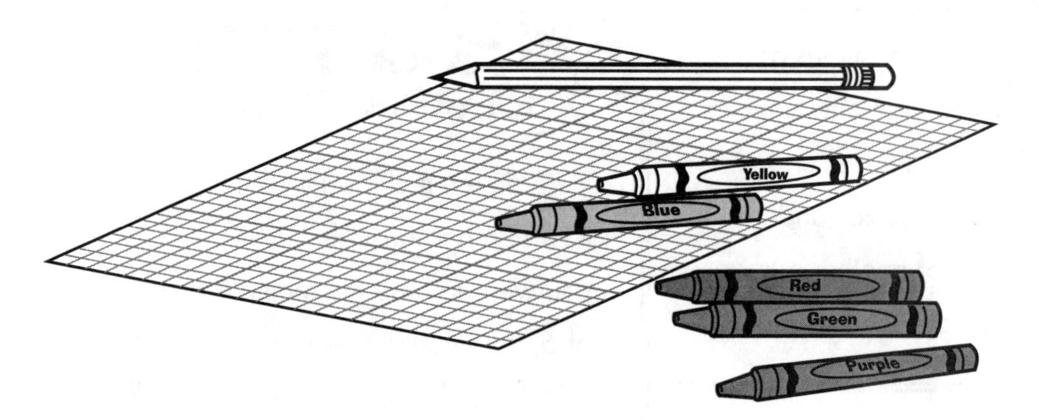

4. Exchange your creation with a friend and figure out each other's pictures. For example, hidden in the grid shown are the multiples of 4. Color the squares to find the hidden picture.

3	24	7	32	10	12	6	16
73	32	15	36	46	36	49	20
18	4	21	40	22	16	26	28
66	12	28	16	63	4	12	32
21	81	19	28	99	17	15	8
67	39	5	24	42	34	31	28
14	1	9	4	29	61	90	8
23	17	19	20	55	35	7	40

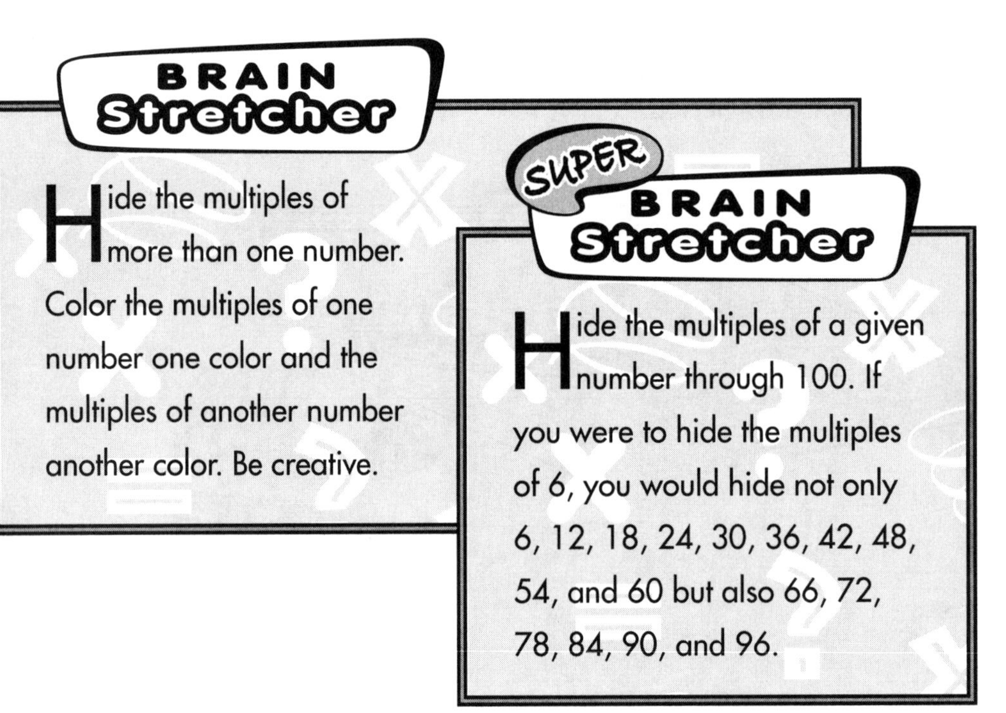

Buzz-Bizz

Playing this noisy game for two or more players will help you learn the multiples of numbers in the multiplication times tables.

Game Rules

1. The players agree on a buzz number. The buzz number can be any number from 2 to 9.
2. The players take turns counting from 1 to 100 or until someone makes a mistake.
3. As player 1 counts, the other players shout, "Buzz!" whenever the number is a multiple of the buzz number.
4. Players shout, "Bizz!" whenever the number contains the buzz number.
5. Players shout, "Buzz-bizz!" (or "Bizz-buzz!"—it really doesn't matter) whenever the number is a multiple of the chosen number and also contains the buzz number.

6. If player 1 makes a mistake and shouts out a wrong number, or if the other players shout, "Buzz!" "Bizz!" or "Buzz-bizz!" at the wrong time, that player earns a letter from the word *BUZZ*. A new buzz number is selected and a new round begins.
7. The first person to earn all of the letters in the word *BUZZ* loses the game. Does it sound confusing? It is, but Buzz-Bizz is easy to learn and lots of fun! For example, this would be the correct sequence of answers if the buzz number were 6: 1, 2, 3, 4, 5, Buzz-bizz! 7, 8, 9, 10, 11, Buzz! 13, 14, 15, Bizz! 17, Buzz! 19, 20, 21, 22, 23, Bizz-buzz! 25, Bizz! 27, 28, 29, Buzz! . . . You get the idea. Since you don't need any equipment, you can play Buzz-Bizz in the car, on the playground, or anywhere.

28

Multiplication Grid

Use a multiplication grid to practice all of the multiplication tables.

MATERIALS

paper
pencil
ruler

Procedure

1. Copy the multiplication grid shown, which represents all of the multiplication tables. Some of the products have been filled in for you.

x	0	1	2	3	4	5	6	7	8	9	10
0											
1	0										
2			4								
3										27	
4				12							
5						25					
6		6			24						
7									56		
8							48				
9								63			
10			20								

2. To find the products of the empty squares, multiply a number in the top row by a number in the first column. Where the row and column intersect, write the answer to the problem.

SUPER MULTIPLICATION GRID

Make a multiplication grid with fourteen rows and fourteen columns. To fill in the products, multiply any number from 0 to 12 by any number from 0 to 12.

IV

Becoming Marvelous at Multiplication

Now that you know your multiplication tables, you can do all sorts of things with multiplication. This section uses fun activities to teach you how to solve more advanced multiplication problems. You'll learn about some of the rules of multiplication, and the difference between primes and multiples. You'll also amaze your friends by doing complicated multiplication problems in your head. When you're done, you'll be a multiplication master!

29 License Plate Multiplication

Multiply the numbers on license plates to learn some of the rules of multiplication.

MATERIALS

- cars with license plates
- friend

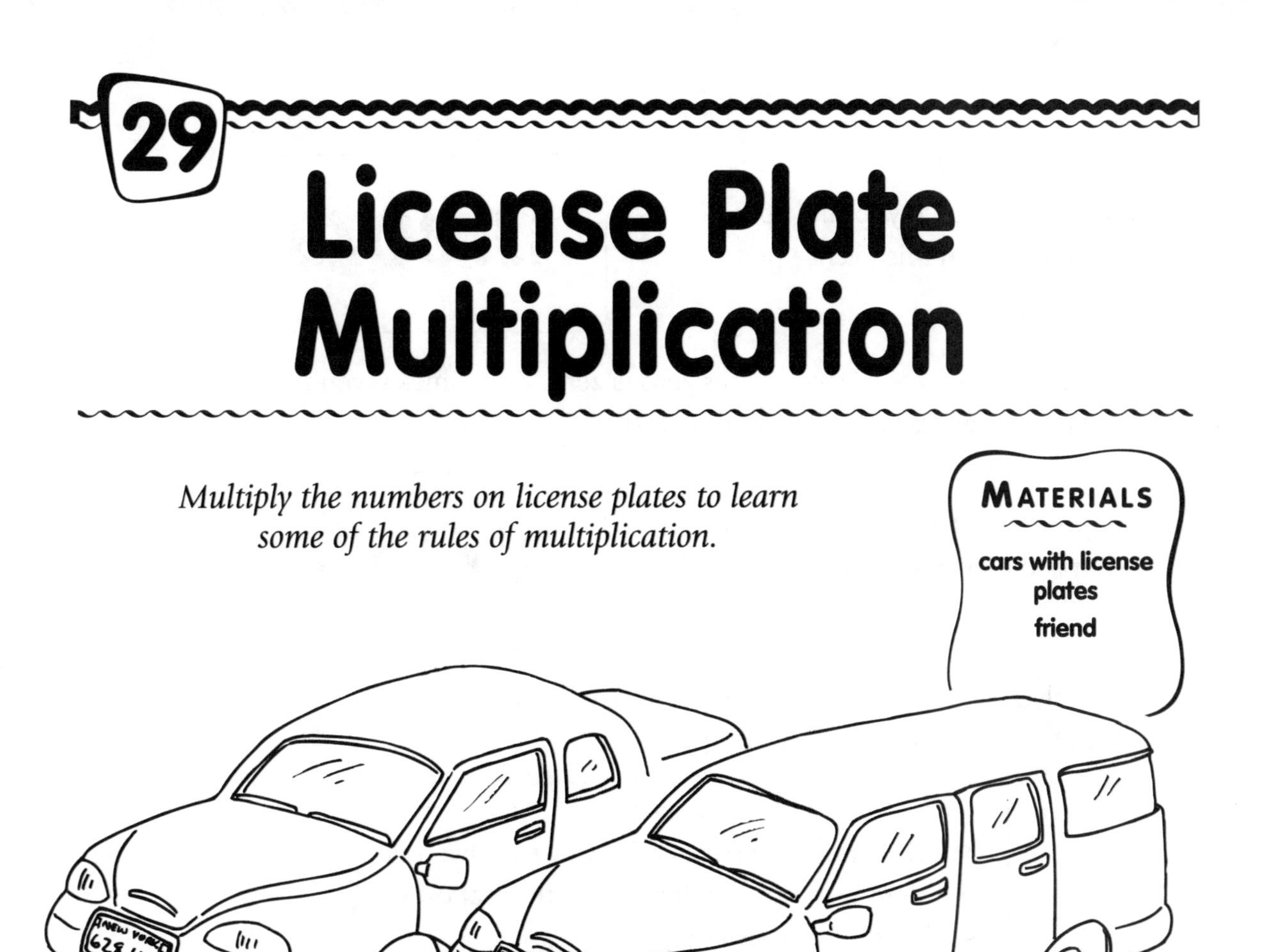

Procedure

1. Any time you are riding in a car (or even in a parking lot), pick a license plate and multiply the numbers on it. Suppose you see a license plate like this one. What is the product of all the digits?

Multiply $2 \times 4 \times 8$. Multiply the first two digits: $2 \times 4 = 8$. Then multiply that product by the third digit: $8 \times 8 = 64$. The product of the digits on the license plate is 64.

2. What do you get if you multiply the numbers on this license plate?

Multiply 3 × 0 × 7 × 8. Three times zero is zero. Zero times seven is zero. Zero times eight is zero. The product is 0.

3. Suppose you saw this license plate. What is the product of all the digits?

Multiply 2 × 1 × 7 × 3. Two times one is two, times seven is fourteen, times three is forty-two. The product is 42.

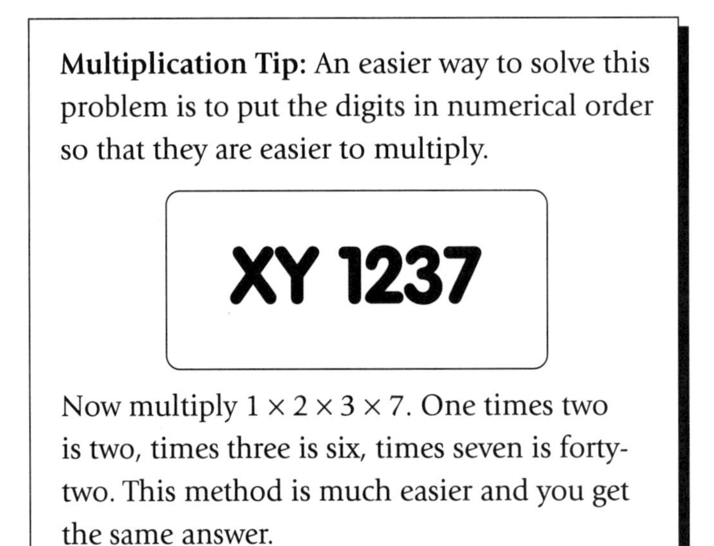

Multiplication Tip: An easier way to solve this problem is to put the digits in numerical order so that they are easier to multiply.

XY 1237

Now multiply 1 × 2 × 3 × 7. One times two is two, times three is six, times seven is forty-two. This method is much easier and you get the same answer.

4. Now that you know how to figure out the product of the numbers on a license plate, you can make License Plate Multiplication a game to play with a friend. Whenever you are in the car with a friend, see who is the first person to find the following five license plates:

A license plate where the product of the numbers is 0.
A license plate where the product is an even number.
A license plate where the product is an odd number.
A license plate where the product is greater than 50.
A license plate where the product is less than 25.

The first player to find all five license plates is the winner.

When you multiply 3 × 2, the answer is the same as when you multiply 2 × 3. Three times two and two times three are both six. The order in which you multiply two numbers doesn't make a difference. This rule is known as the "commutative property of multiplication."

The order in which you group a series of multiplied numbers also doesn't make a difference. The product of 6 × 4 multiplied by 2 is the same as 6 multiplied by the product of 4 × 2. If you were to write this mathematically, it would be $(6 \times 4) \times 2 = 6 \times (4 \times 2)$, where the numbers within parentheses are multiplied first. The "associative property of multiplication" is another rule, which says you can group the numbers you are going to multiply any way you like.

Because of these two rules, the commutative property of multiplication and the associative property of multiplication, when you multiply the digits of a license plate, you can multiply them in any order you want. You'll always get the same answer. So you can group and multiply the numbers in any order that is easiest for you.

Amazing Multiples

Use this exercise to learn which numbers are multiples of other numbers. You'll also learn about prime numbers.

MATERIALS

- crayons or colored markers: black, red, green, blue, yellow
- white poster board or large sheet of newsprint

Procedure

1. Write "Amazing Multiples" in black at the top of a poster board. Below that and in black, write the numbers from 1 to 100 in rows of ten. Make the numbers large enough to fill up the entire board. Your poster board should look like the one here.

Amazing Multiples

1	2	3	4	5	6	7	8	9	10
11	12	13	14	15	16	17	18	19	20
21	22	23	24	25	26	27	28	29	30
31	32	33	34	35	36	37	38	39	40
41	42	43	44	45	46	47	48	49	50
51	52	53	54	55	56	57	58	59	60
61	62	63	64	65	66	67	68	69	70
71	72	73	74	75	76	77	78	79	80
81	82	83	84	85	86	87	88	89	90
91	92	93	94	95	96	97	98	99	100

2. In red, circle the number 2. Two is the first prime number. You're going to circle all the prime numbers. A prime number is a number that is only divisible by (a multiple of) itself and 1.
3. Now put a red slash, /, through all the multiples of 2. Start with 4, since $2 \times 2 = 4$. Then put a red slash through 6, 8, 10, 12, 14, and so on. (In fact, you have to put a red slash through all the even numbers, since all the even numbers are multiples of 2.)
4. In green, circle the number 3. (Three is also a prime number.) Then put a green back slash,\, through all the multiples of 3. Start with 6 since $3 \times 2 = 6$, then mark 9, 12, 15, 18, 21, 24, and so on (every third number).
5. In red, underline the number 4; don't circle it. Four is not a prime number. Four is a multiple of itself and 1, but it is also a multiple of 2. Then starting with 8, underline in red every other number that has a red slash through it. These numbers are the multiples of 4: 8, 12, 16, 20, 24, 28, 32, and so on. (The reason you use red to underline the multiples of 4 is that they are also the multiples of 2.)
6. In blue, circle the number 5. Five is a prime number. Then put a blue dash, —, through all the multiples of 5. Start with 10, since $5 \times 2 = 10$, then mark 15, 20, 25, 30, 35, 40, 45, 50, and so on (every fifth number, or every number that ends in a 5 or a 0).
7. Six is not a prime number. Six is a multiple of 1, 2, 3, and 6. You don't have to mark the multiples of 6 because they are already marked. They are the numbers that have both a red slash and a green back slash through them. These are multiples of both 2 and 3, because $2 \times 3 = 6$. Find them. They should be 6, 12, 18, 24, and so on.
8. Seven is a prime number. In yellow, circle the number 7. Then put a vertical yellow line, |, through all the multiples of 7. Start with 14, since $7 \times 2 = 14$, then mark every seventh number: 14, 21, 28, 35, 42, 49, 56, 63, 70, 77, 84, 91, and 98.

9. Eight is not a prime number. Eight is a multiple of both 2 and 4. Put a red horizontal line over the number 8; don't circle it. Then put a red line over every other number with a red line under it, or every other multiple of 4. These numbers are the multiples of 8: 16, 24, 32, 40, and so on.
10. Nine is not a prime number. Nine is a multiple of 3. In green, put a vertical line to the left of the number 9; don't circle it. Then put a green line to the left of every third number that has a green back slash through it, or every third multiple of 3. These are the multiples of 9: 18, 27, 36, 45, 54, 63, 72, 81, 90, and 99.
11. Ten is not a prime number. Ten is a multiple of 1, 2, and 5. You don't have to mark the multiples of 10 because they are already marked. They are the numbers that have both a red slash and a blue dash through them. These are multiples of both 2 and 5, because 2 x 5 = 10.
12. The numbers you circled: 2, 3, 5, and 7 are prime numbers. The other prime numbers less than 100 are: 11, 13, 17, 19, 23, 29, 31, 37, 41, 43, 47, 53, 57, 59, 61, 67, 71, 73, 79, 83, 87, 89, 91, and 97.

Practice Makes Perfect

You can practice reciting the multiples of different numbers by using this grid. It's color-coded to help you. Learning multiples will help you learn your multiplication tables.

To practice reciting the multiples of 2, read all the numbers with a red slash through them.

To practice reciting the multiples of 3, read all the numbers with a green back slash through them.

To practice reciting the multiples of 4, read all the numbers with a red line under them.

To practice reciting the multiples of 5, read all the numbers with a blue dash through them.

To practice reciting the multiples of 6, read all the numbers that have both a red slash and a green back slash through them.

To practice reciting the multiples of 7, read all the numbers with a vertical yellow line through them.

To practice reciting the multiples of 8, read all the numbers with a red line over them.

To practice reciting the multiples of 9, read all the numbers with a vertical green line to the left of them.

To practice reciting the multiples of 10, read all the numbers with a red slash and blue dash through them.

31

What's the Problem?

Now that you know the multiplication tables, it's time to learn how to multiply a two-digit number by a one-digit number.

Materials

pencil
paper
calculator

Procedure

1. The easiest way to multiply a two-digit number by a one-digit number is to break the problem down into two separate multiplication problems. How do you multiply 34×2? Break it down into two separate multiplication problems. First multiply 4×2,

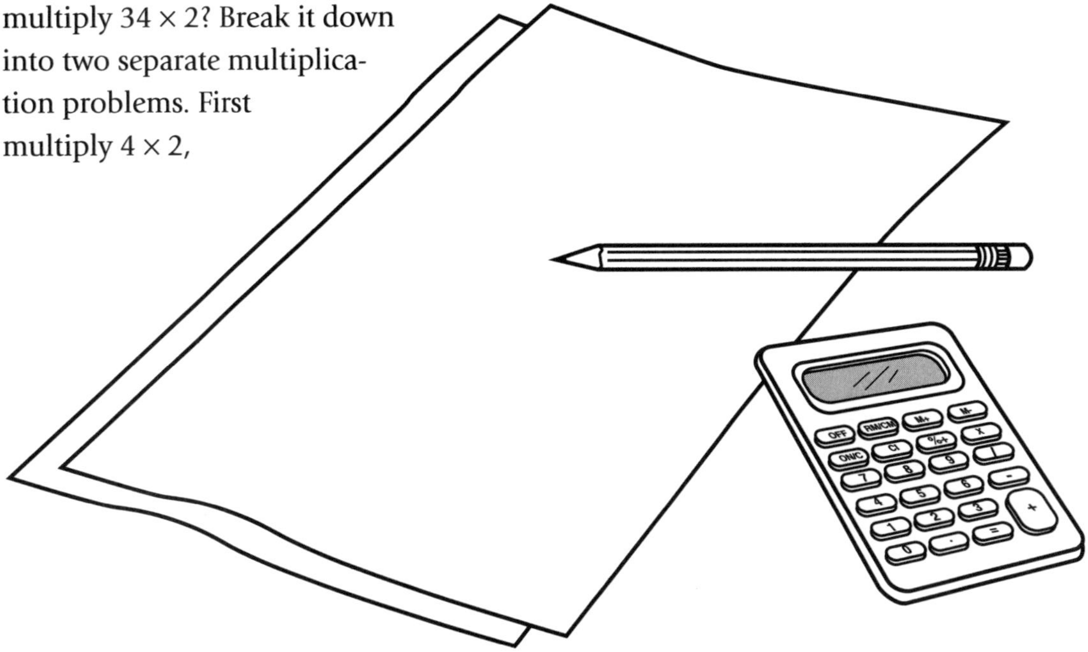

which is 8. (Always start with the digit on the right, in the ones place. You'll see why this is important later on.) Place the 8 under the 4 and 2.

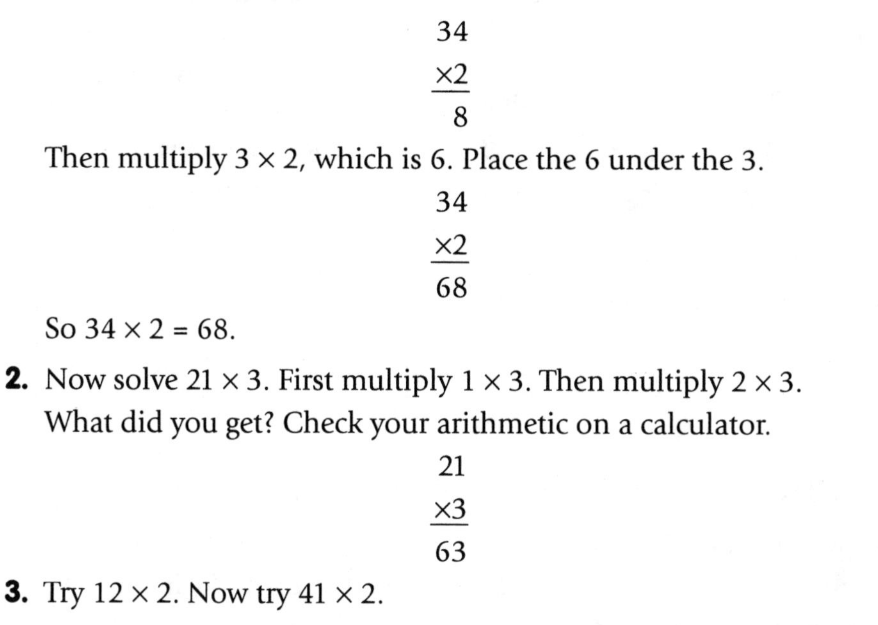

$$\begin{array}{r} 34 \\ \underline{\times 2} \\ 8 \end{array}$$

Then multiply 3×2, which is 6. Place the 6 under the 3.

$$\begin{array}{r} 34 \\ \underline{\times 2} \\ 68 \end{array}$$

So $34 \times 2 = 68$.

2. Now solve 21×3. First multiply 1×3. Then multiply 2×3. What did you get? Check your arithmetic on a calculator.

$$\begin{array}{r} 21 \\ \underline{\times 3} \\ 63 \end{array}$$

3. Try 12×2. Now try 41×2.

4. What is 46×5? First multiply 6×5, which is 30. Put the 0 under the 6 and 5, but put the 3 above the 4. The 3 is three 10's, so it goes in the tens place.

$$\begin{array}{r} 3 \\ 46 \\ \underline{\times 5} \\ 0 \end{array}$$

Next multiply 4×5, which is 20, and add the 3 from the tens place to get 23. Put the 23 under the 4.

$$\begin{array}{r} 46 \\ \underline{\times 5} \\ 230 \end{array}$$

5. Try 38×8. Try 27×6. Now try 32×4. When you can multiply a two-digit number by a one-digit number, you are ready to play What's the Problem?

Game Preparation

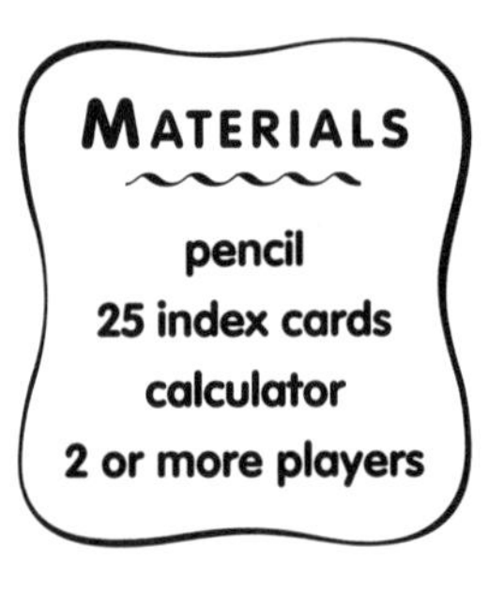

Write one of the following numbers on each of twenty-five index cards:

210	**243**	**252**	**176**	**369**
216	**88**	**312**	**343**	**648**
112	**539**	**396**	**162**	**128**
704	**96**	**160**	**147**	**588**
125	**144**	**220**	**102**	**198**

Game Rules

1. Place the stack of index cards facedown in the middle of the table.
2. One player turns over the top card and the other players try to figure out a multiplication problem that could result in that answer. For example, if 176 is turned over, the true problem could be any of the following:

   What is 88×2?
   What is 44×4?
   What is 22×8?
3. When a player suggests a problem, use the calculator to check the results. The first player to figure out a true problem wins the card. The first player to win three cards wins the game.

BRAIN Stretcher

Even though you read from left to right, you multiply a two-digit number by a one-digit number from right to left. Why? Individual numerals have different values depending on where they are placed in a number. This is called their "place value." For example, in the number 5,231, the 5 stands for five thousands. The 5 is in the thousands place. In the number 544, the 5 stands for five hundreds. The 5 is in the hundreds place. In the number 51, the 5 stands for five tens. The 5 is in the tens place. And the number 5 alone stands for five ones. The 5 is in the ones place. When you multiply any two numbers, you always start with the number in the ones place.

Flashing Factors

This game will give you practice multiplying numbers and finding factors that have common products. This is called "factoring."

MATERIALS

pencil
40 index cards
calculator
2 players

Game Preparation

Write one of the following multiplication problems on each of forty index cards:

2 x 6	**4 x 6**	**5 x 12**	**8 x 9**
2 x 8	**4 x 7**	**5 x 20**	**8 x 10**
2 x 10	**4 x 8**	**6 x 7**	**8 x 12**
2 x 12	**4 x 9**	**6 x 8**	**8 x 25**
3 x 4	**4 x 10**	**6 x 9**	**9 x 10**
3 x 6	**4 x 12**	**6 x 10**	**9 x 12**
3 x 8	**4 x 20**	**6 x 12**	**10 x 10**
3 x 10	**5 x 6**	**7 x 8**	**10 x 12**
3 x 12	**5 x 8**	**7 x 10**	**25 x 4**
4 x 5	**5 x 10**	**7 x 12**	**10 x 100**

Game Rules

1. Shuffle the cards and place them facedown in the center of the table.
2. Player 1 turns the top index card over and player 2 solves the multiplication problem in his or her head. Player 2 then tries to win the card by thinking of another multiplication problem that uses two different factors but has the same answer as the problem on the card. For example, if the problem on the card is 4×9, another problem could be 12×3 or 6×6. The common product for all factors is 36.
3. Players *cannot* use the number 1 in any problem.
4. If a player suggests an incorrect problem, the other player wins the card. The game continues until all cards are played. The player who has won the most cards is the winner. Use the calculator if you need to check the answers.

SUPER FLASHING FACTORS

Super Flashing Factors is played in the same way as Flashing Factors, except with three players. If player 3 can think of a different pair of correct factors after player 2, player 3 wins the card. Whoever thinks of the last possible pair of correct factors wins the card. For example, if the problem on the card is 25×4, player 2 could suggest 10×10 and win the card. Then player 3 could suggest 50×2 and win the card away from player 2. Finally, player 1 could suggest 20×5 and win the card from player 3. There are no more ways to factor 100, so player 1 wins the card.

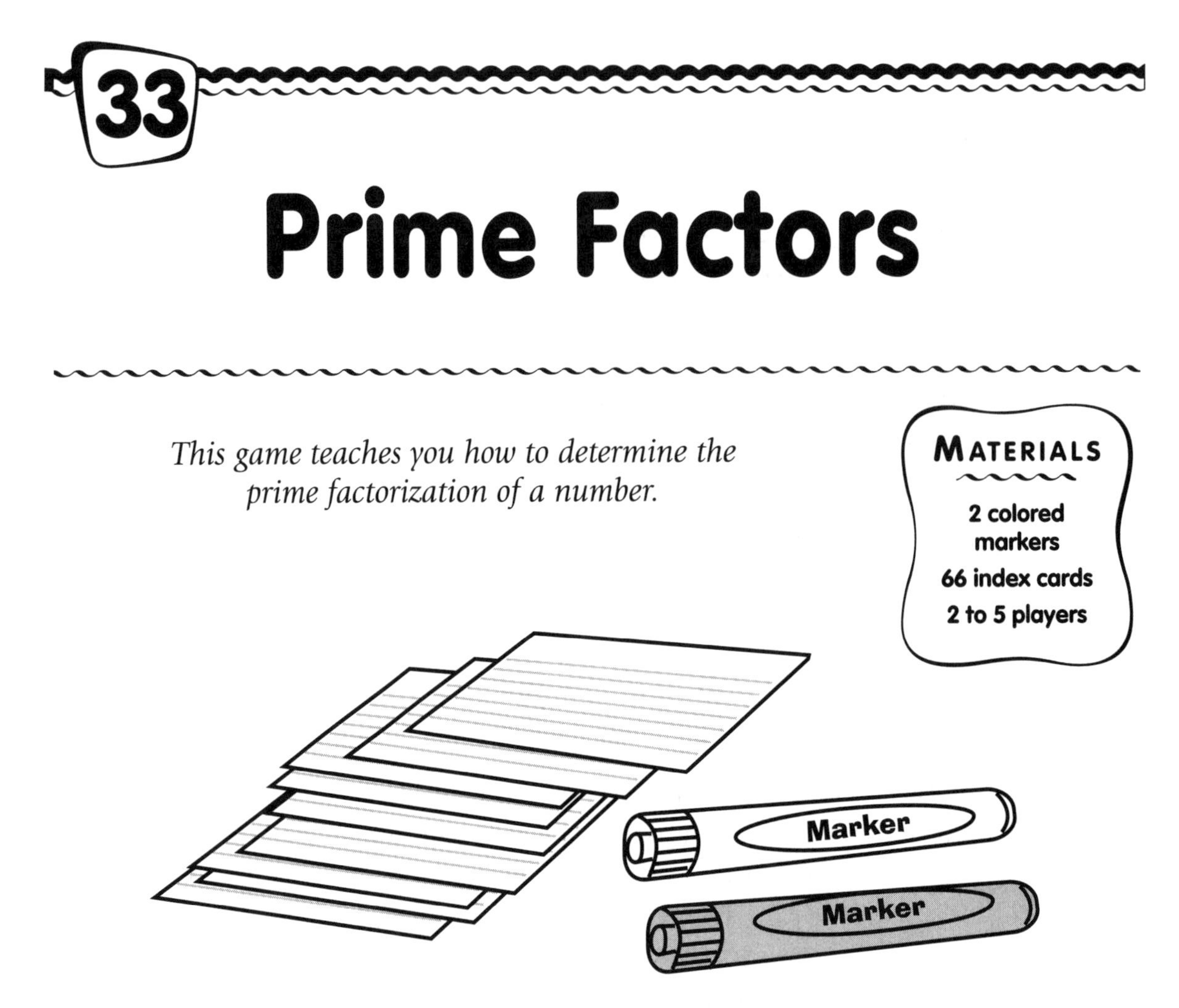

33 Prime Factors

This game teaches you how to determine the prime factorization of a number.

Materials

2 colored markers

66 index cards

2 to 5 players

Game Preparation

1. Using one of the colored markers, write "Multiples" on one side of sixteen index cards. On the other side of each, write one of the following numbers: 8, 10, 12, 14, 16, 18, 20, 24, 28, 30, 35, 36, 40, 42, 45, 50. These numbers are called multiples because they can be formed by multiplying two or more numbers.
2. Use the second colored marker to write "Prime" on one side of the fifty remaining index cards. Write a 2 on the other side of twenty-five of the cards, a 3 on ten cards, a 5 on ten cards, and a 7 on five cards. The

numbers 2, 3, 5, and 7 are all prime numbers. (You learned about prime numbers in Chapter 30.) The numbers 2, 3, 5, and 7 aren't multiples of any number besides themselves and 1.

Game Rules

1. Place the stack of multiples cards facedown in the center of the table. Turn the top three cards over and place them to the right of the stack.

2. Now deal each player five prime cards. Place the rest of the prime cards facedown to the right of the multiples cards.

3. Player 1 draws a card from the prime pile and adds it to the prime cards in his or her hand. Then he looks for a combination of prime cards that are factors of one of the faceup multiples cards. For example, if one of the multiples cards is 35, the player's prime cards need to be 5 and 7, because $5 \times 7 = 35$. If the multiples card is 16, the prime cards need to be four 2's, because $2 \times 2 \times 2 \times 2 = 16$.

4. If player 1 has the combination of prime cards, he or she places them in a group on top of the multiples card and places all these cards in front of himself or herself. A new multiples card is turned over to replace the played card.
5. If the player does not have the combination, he or she keeps the drawn prime card and player 2 takes a turn.
6. The game continues until all multiples cards are played. The player who has made the most combinations wins the game.

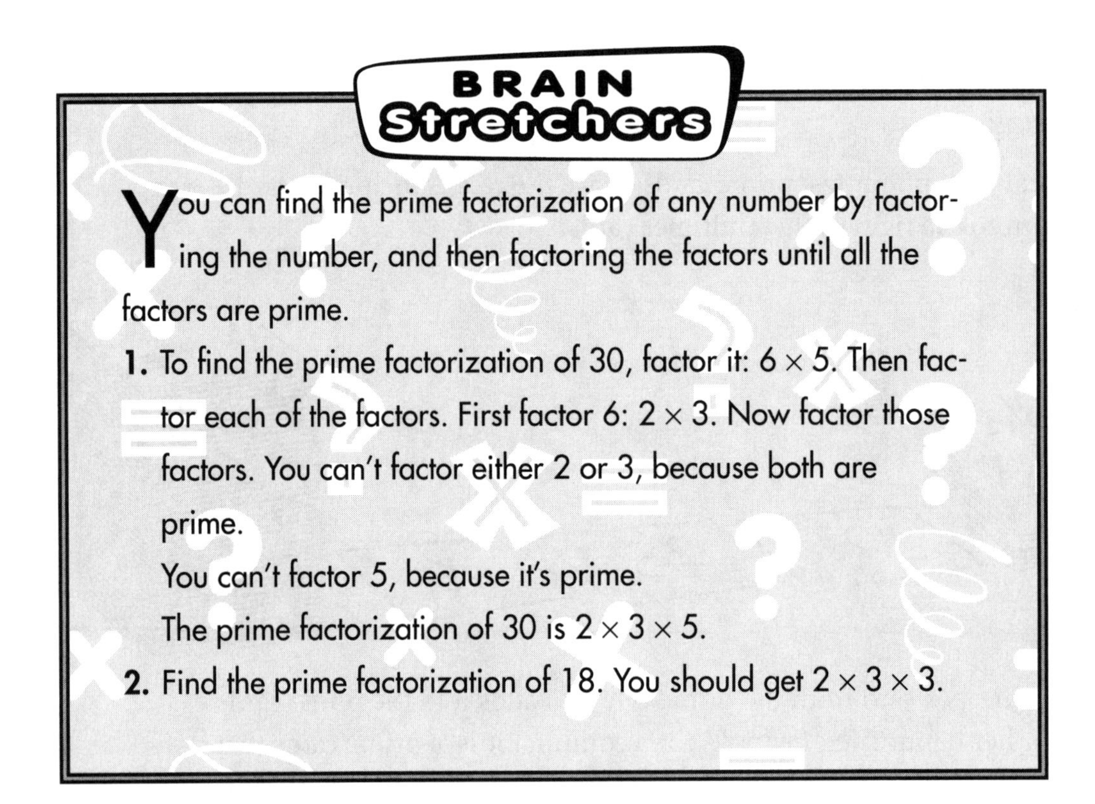

BRAIN Stretchers

You can find the prime factorization of any number by factoring the number, and then factoring the factors until all the factors are prime.

1. To find the prime factorization of 30, factor it: 6×5. Then factor each of the factors. First factor 6: 2×3. Now factor those factors. You can't factor either 2 or 3, because both are prime.
   You can't factor 5, because it's prime.
   The prime factorization of 30 is $2 \times 3 \times 5$.
2. Find the prime factorization of 18. You should get $2 \times 3 \times 3$.

Every number has only one prime factorization.

1. Factor the number 36:

$$36 = 4 \times 9$$
$$4 = 2 \times 2, \text{ and } 9 = 3 \times 3$$
$$36 = 2 \times 2 \times 3 \times 3$$

All of these numbers are prime, so $2 \times 2 \times 3 \times 3$ is the prime factorization of 36.

2. The number 36 can be factored another way, using a different factor pair to start: $36 = 3 \times 12$. Three is a prime number and cannot be factored. Factor 12: 3×4. Three is a prime number. Factor 4: 2×2. Two is a prime number, so again the prime factorization of 36 is $3 \times 3 \times 2 \times 2$.
3. Find the prime factorization of 50 two different ways. The answer should be the same no matter how you find it.
4. Find the prime factorization of 24 two different ways. Are your answers the same? They should be!

Prime Solitaire

Find the prime factorization of random numbers.

Materials

dice

1 or more players

Game Rules

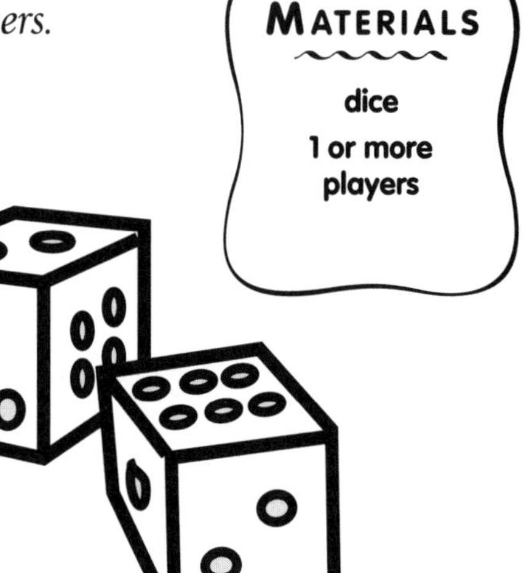

1. Roll the dice. Use the numbers on the dice to make two numbers by making one of the numbers the tens digit and the other the ones digit, and then switching the places. For example, if you rolled a 5 and a 3, the numbers would be 53 and 35.
2. Find the prime factorization of both of the numbers. The number 53 is prime, so it cannot be factored. Now factor 35: 7 × 5. Both 7 and 5 are prime, so 7 × 5 is the prime factorization of 35.
3. Roll the dice and see what other numbers you come up with.

SUPER PRIME SOLITAIRE

Roll the dice and put a 1 in front of the numbers. Now try to find the prime factorization of these three-digit numbers.

35

Engaging Exponents

This activity will teach you about exponents and how to use them.

MATERIALS

5 pieces of paper

Procedure

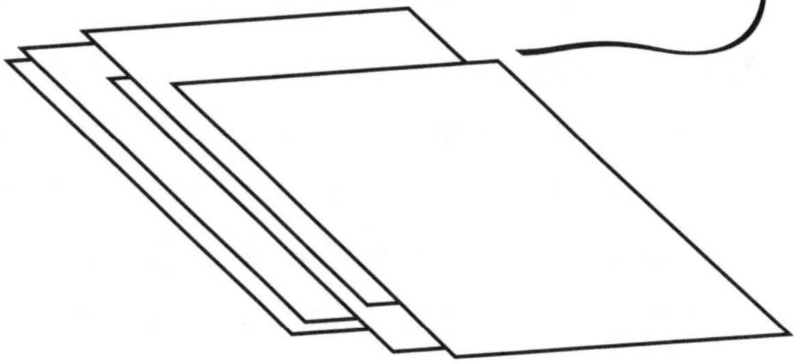

1. Take the first piece of paper, fold it in half, then unfold it. The paper should contain two sections.

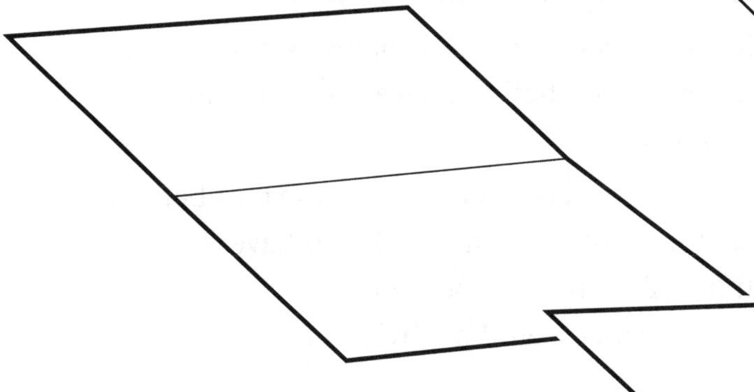

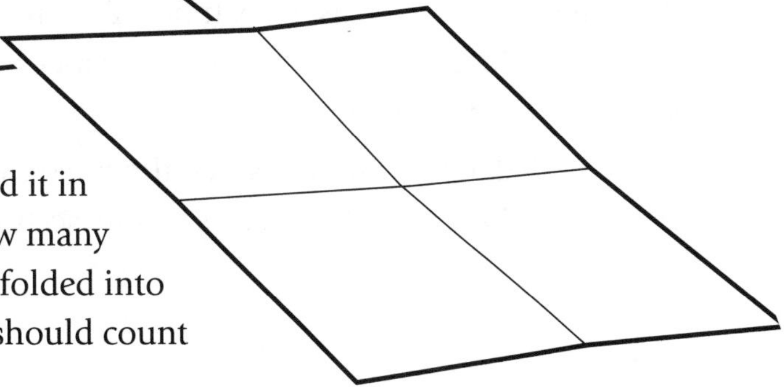

2. Take the second piece of paper, fold it in half, then fold it in half again. How many sections do you think the paper is folded into now? Unfold it and find out. You should count four sections.

3. Take a third piece of paper, fold it in half, fold it in half again, then fold it in half again. How many sections do you think the paper is folded into now? Unfold it and count them. You should see eight sections.

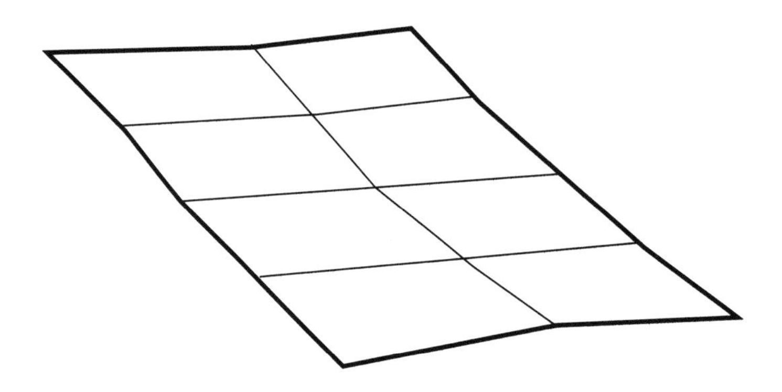

4. Every time you fold a piece of paper, in half, you double the number of sections it contains. Amazing. Fold the fourth piece of paper in half, and in half again, and again, and again. You will have sixteen sections.
5. Now before you fold the fifth piece of paper, guess how many sections there will be if you fold it in half five times. After you have guessed, fold and unfold the paper to check your answer.
6. Without folding a piece of paper, you should be able to guess the number of sections if you fold it in half six times. To figure it out all you have to do is multiply 2 times itself six times. The answer would be $2 \times 2 \times 2 \times 2 \times 2 \times 2$, which is 64. The paper would be divided into sixty-four different sections.
7. If you folded a paper in half seven times, you would get $2 \times 2 \times 2 \times 2 \times 2 \times 2 \times 2$, or 128 separate sections.

BRAIN Stretchers

1. Mathematicians got tired of writing so many 2's in a row, so they developed something called "exponential notation." Instead of writing $2 \times 2 \times 2 \times 2 \times 2 \times 2$, they write 2^6, which means the same thing. The 2 is called the "base" and the 6, which is written smaller and higher, is called the "exponent." The notation 2^6 is read as two to the sixth power, and means multiply 2 by itself six times.

   The notation 3^4 is read as three to the fourth power. Three is the base and four is the exponent. It means 3 times itself four times, or $3 \times 3 \times 3 \times 3$. So $3^4 = 81$.

   The notation 5^2 is read as five to the second power or five squared. Five squared is the same as 5×5 and is equal to 25.

   Try to solve these exponential notations:

   What is 3^3?

   What is 2^3?

   What is 6^2?

   What is 4^4?

   Did you get 27, 8, 36, and 256? Congratulations!

2. The multiples of 10, or "powers of 10," are commonly written in exponential notation. Watch as these powers of 10 are changed to what is called "standard notation."

   $10^1 = 10$

   $10^2 = 100$

   $10^3 = 1{,}000$

   $10^4 = 10{,}000$

$10^5 = 100,000$

$10^6 = 1,000,000$

$10^7 = 10,000,000$

Did you notice that the number of 0's after the 1 is the same as the exponent? Powers of 10 are easy to change to standard notation. Just write a 1 and add the correct number of 0's.

Can you change the following numbers to standard notation?

10^{12}

10^{20}

Can you write the following numbers in exponential notation?

1000000000000

1000000000000000

If you understand exponents, you can understand what is called "scientific notation." Scientists developed scientific notation as a shortcut for writing long numbers. If you wanted to write 3,000,000,000 in scientific notation, you could write 3×10^9. If you wanted to write 400 in scientific notation, you could write 4×10^2. Write the following numbers in scientific notation: five thousand, 7 million, 6 billion, and 3 trillion.

36 Mental Multiplication Tricks

How would you like to be able to solve simple and not-so-simple multiplication problems in your head? You could solve 28 × 2, or 99 × 6, or even 105 × 7. Sound impossible? Not really. Once you learn a few little tricks, you'll amaze your friends and even yourself.

MATERIALS

calculator

Procedure

1. Start by learning certain large multiplication tables. The 100 times table is the easiest to learn. It's 1 × 100 = 100, 2 × 100 = 200, 3 × 100 = 300, 4 × 100 = 400, 5 × 100 = 500, 6 × 100 = 600, 7 × 100 = 700, 8 × 100 = 800, 9 × 100 = 900, 10 × 100 = 1,000.
2. Now suppose you wanted to multiply 107 × 5. You could do it the long way. Or you could break it down: 100 × 5 = 500 and 7 × 5 = 35. Then add the two answers to get 535. The trick is to multiply by 100 first, since you know the 100 times table perfectly.

107×5= 100×5+7×5=500+35=535

3. Try this problem: What is 97×3? Since 97 is only 3 less than 100, you could multiply 100×3 to get 300, then multiply the difference between 97 and 100 ($100 - 97 = 3$) by 3 and subtract that from 300. Since $3 \times 3 = 9$, you subtract 9 from 300 to get 291. So $97 \times 3 = 291$.

4. Can you solve these problems in your head? Use a calculator to check your answers. Remember to multiply by 100 first.

$101 \times 2 =$

$110 \times 7 =$

$111 \times 3 =$

$109 \times 6 =$

What about these?

$99 \times 2 =$

$98 \times 5 =$

$91 \times 4 =$

A similar technique can be used for numbers close to 25. First you have to learn the 25 times table. This table is easy to remember if you imagine you're counting quarters. One quarter is 25¢, so $1 \times 25 = 25$. Two quarters are 50¢, so $2 \times 25 = 50$. Three quarters are 75¢, so $3 \times 25 = 75$. Four quarters are 100¢ or $1, so $4 \times 25 = 100$. The rest of the table is $5 \times 25 = 125$, $6 \times 25 = 150$, $7 \times 25 = 175$, $8 \times 25 = 200$, $9 \times 25 = 225$, and $10 \times 25 = 250$.

Now that you know the 25 times table, try doing these problems mentally.

1. What is 27×3? Since 27 is 2 more than 25, start by multiplying 25×3, which is 75. Now take the 2 you dropped off the 25 and multiply that by 3: $2 \times 3 = 6$. Now add 75 and 6 to get 81. So $27 \times 3 = 81$.
2. What is 23×5? Since 23 is 2 less than 25, start by multiplying 25×5, which is 125. Now take the 2 you added onto the 25 and multiply that by 5. $2 \times 5 = 10$. Now subtract 10 from 125 to get 115. So $23 \times 5 = 115$.
3. Try to solve these problems in your head. Once you get the hang of it, you should be able to solve problems on your own faster than you can with a calculator.

   What is 24×2?
   What is 26×2?
   What is 28×5?
   What is 22×4?

Guesstimating

This game will give you practice guesstimating (a combination of guessing and estimating) the answers to multiplication problems.

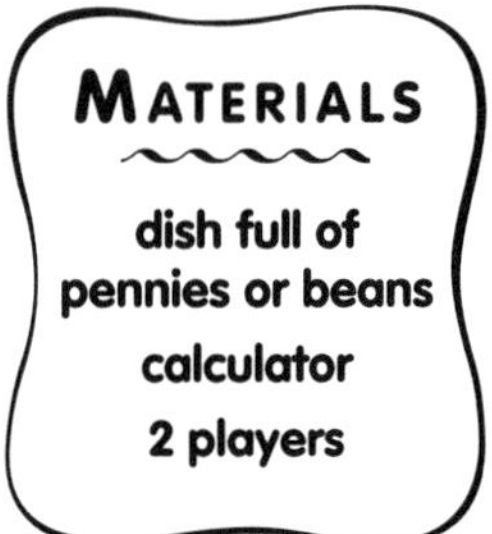

Game Rules

1. Player 1 takes a handful of pennies, counts them out loud, and replaces them in the dish.
2. Player 2 then takes a handful of pennies, counts them out loud, and replaces them in the dish.

3. Both players try to guess the product of the two numbers.
4. Solve the problem on a calculator. The player who comes closer to the actual product earns 1 point. The first player to earn 10 points wins the game.

One way to estimate the product of two numbers is to round the two numbers. If player 1 picked seventeen pennies from the dish and player 2 picked 32, round 17 to 20 and 32 to 30. Multiply 20×30 together in your head: $20 \times 30 = 600$, which means that 600 would be a good guess. Now multiply 17×32 using paper and pencil or a calculator to find the actual product: $17 \times 32 = 544$. So 600 was a pretty good guess.

Guesstimating is a good way to check the answers to your multiplication problems.

Three by Three

This game will show you how to multiply a three-digit number by a three-digit number.

MATERIALS

playing cards
pencil
paper
calculator
2 players

Game Preparation

Remove the tens, jacks, queens, and jokers from a standard deck of playing cards. Be sure to leave the kings in the deck. The deck should now contain forty cards.

Game Rules

1. Shuffle the deck of cards and place the stack face-down on the table.
2. Player 1 turns the top three cards over. These cards make up the first number in the multiplication problem. For example, if player 1 turns over the 3 of diamonds, the 6 of clubs, and the 2 of hearts, then the first number in his or her multiplication problem is 362.
3. Player 1 turns another three cards over to get the second number in the multiplication problem. For example, if the next three cards are the 4 of

hearts, the 7 of spades, and the king of spades, the second number in his or her multiplication problem is 470. (Kings count as 0's, aces as 1's.)

4. Player 1 writes down his or her multiplication problem but does not solve it yet.
5. Player 2 turns over six cards and determines his or her multiplication problem in the same way.
6. Both players race to see who can solve his or her multiplication problem first. Answers are checked with the calculator. The first player to correctly solve the problem wins the round. The first player to win three rounds wins the game.

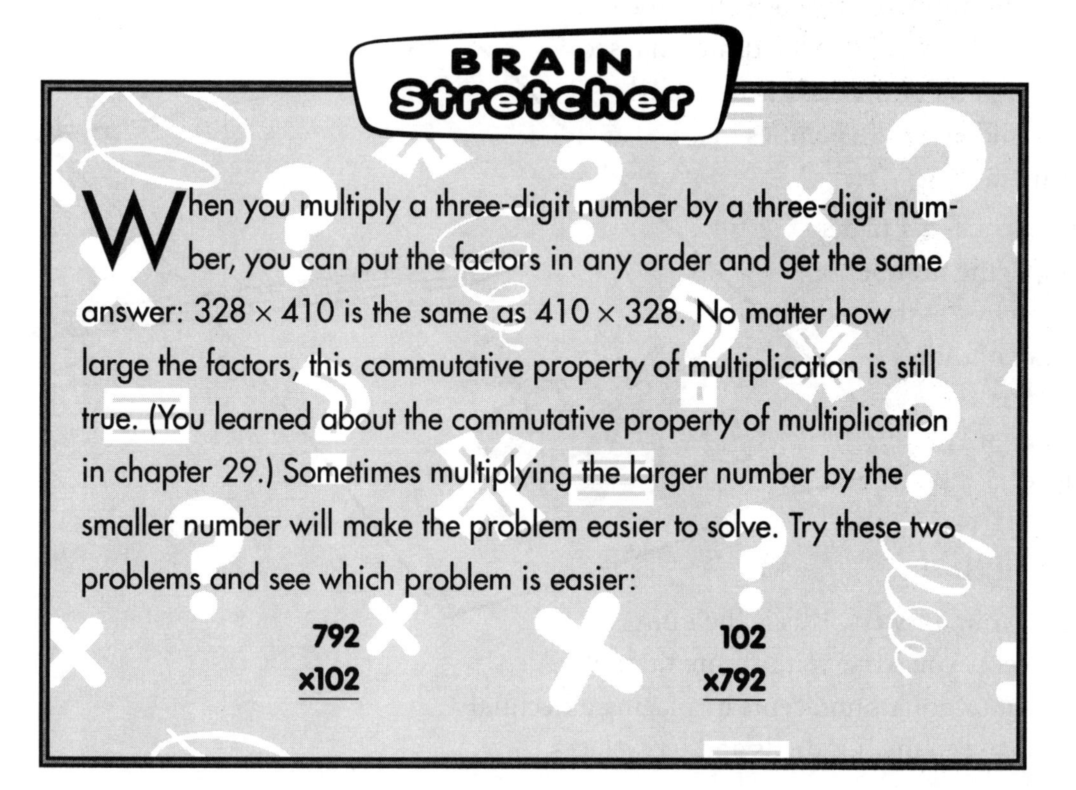

BRAIN Stretcher

When you multiply a three-digit number by a three-digit number, you can put the factors in any order and get the same answer: 328 × 410 is the same as 410 × 328. No matter how large the factors, this commutative property of multiplication is still true. (You learned about the commutative property of multiplication in chapter 29.) Sometimes multiplying the larger number by the smaller number will make the problem easier to solve. Try these two problems and see which problem is easier:

$$\begin{array}{r} 792 \\ \times 102 \\ \hline \end{array} \qquad \begin{array}{r} 102 \\ \times 792 \\ \hline \end{array}$$

39

Handfuls of Change

How do you figure out the value of the change in your pocket?

MATERIALS

Several handfuls of change
pencil
paper

Procedure

1. Place a handful of change on the table. The change should include coins of different value.
2. Sort the coins by value. Place all of the quarters in one group, all of the dimes in a second group, all of the nickels in a third group, and all of the pennies in a fourth group.
3. Using pencil and paper, multiply the number of quarters by 25, the number of dimes by 10, the number of nickels by 5, and the number of pennies by 1.
4. Add all your answers. This is the number of cents you have. If it is more than 99¢, change it to dollars and cents by placing a decimal point between the hundreds and tens places.

For example, say you have five quarters, three dimes, two nickels and four pennies. Multiply the quarters: $5 \times 25 = 125$. Multiply the dimes: $3 \times 10 = 30$. Multiply the nickels: $2 \times 5 = 10$. Multiply the pennies: $1 \times 4 = 4$. Add all the change: $125 + 30 + 10 + 4 = 169$. Change it to dollars and cents: $1.69.

5. Now count three handfuls of change and see which is worth more.

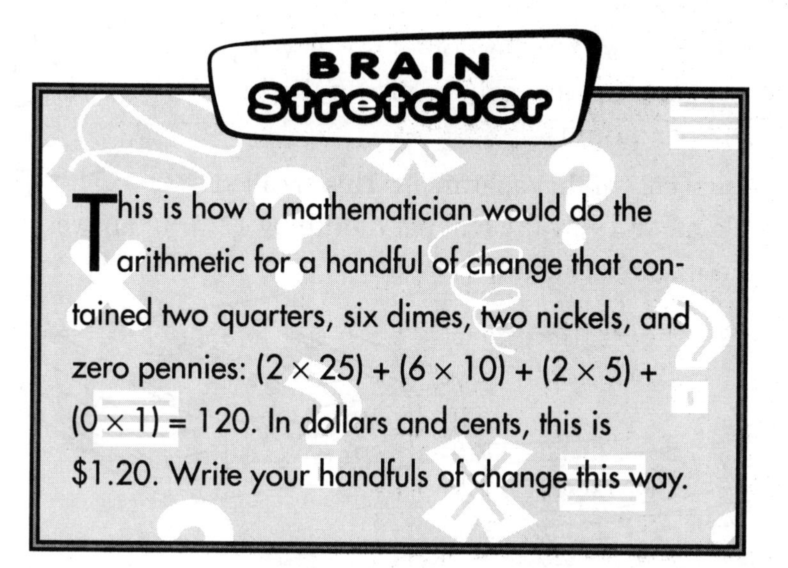

Annualizing

Use this exercise to learn how to annualize the cost of things.

Procedure

1. Look in the "Apartments for Rent" section of the newspaper classifieds. Find an apartment that sounds nice to live in. Write down the rent per month.
2. Figure out the annual cost of that apartment. This is called "annualizing" the rent. Multiply the rent per month by 12. Your answer is the cost of living in that apartment for 1 year.

3. Look up the number of a local hotel in the Yellow Pages under "Hotels."
4. Call the hotel and ask the room rate for 1 night. Now multiply this rate by 365. Your answer is the room rate for 1 year. You have annualized the room rate.
5. Check your answers with a calculator. Which is more expensive, the hotel room or the apartment?

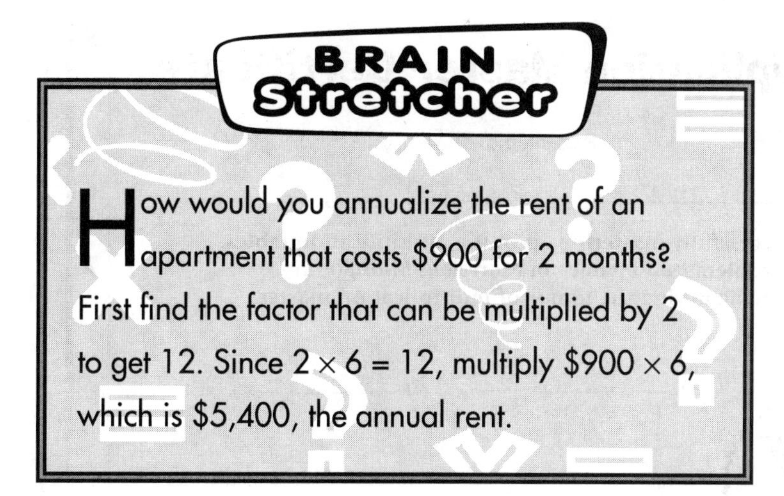

Multiplication Master Certificate

Now that you've mastered all of the multiplication tables, problems, and games in this book, you are officially certified as a multiplication master! Make a photocopy of this certificate, write your name on the copy, and hang it on the wall.

Index